IELTS VOCABULARY 8.5 MASTERCLASS SERIES MEGAPACK: BOOKS 1, 2 & 3

ADVANCED VOCABULARY MASTERCLASS BOOKS

FULL SELF-STUDY COURSE FOR IELTS 8.5 VOCABULARY.

SELF-STUDY IELTS PROGRAM

Contents

BOOK 1

IELTS 8.5
IELTS VOCABULARY MASTERCLASS. PHRASAL VERBS, ESSAY VOCABULARY, GRAPH VOCABULARY & SPEAKING VOCABULARY

IELTS VOCABULARY BOOK

MARC ROCHE

IELTS is a registered trademark of University of Cambridge ESOL, the British Council, and IDP Education Australia.

Topics covered in this book-

IELTS, IELTS Vocabulary, IELTS academic vocabulary, vocabulary IELTS, IELTS book, IELTS General

ABOUT THE AUTHOR

Marc is a teacher, trainer and writer. He has collaborated with organisations such as the British Council, the Royal Melbourne Institute of Technology and University of Technology Sydney among others. Marc has also worked with multinationals such as Nike, GlaxoSmithKline or Bolsas y Mercados.

OTHER BOOKS BY MARC ROCHE

IELTS Writing 9.0 Proficiency

IELTS Vocabulary Masterclass 8.5 (BOOK 1)

IELTS Vocabulary Masterclass 8.5 (BOOK 2)

IELTS Vocabulary Masterclass 8.5 (BOOK 3)

IELTS Vocabulary 8.5 Masterclass Series MegaPack

IELTS Speaking 8.5 Master Plan

IELTS Writing Masterclass 8.5

Grammar for IELTS 8.5 (Book 1)

GET MARC ROCHE'S STARTER LIBRARY FOR FREE

Sign up for exclusive content via email and get an introductory book and lots more, all for free.

Details can be found at the end of the book.

WHY I WROTE THIS IELTS BOOK

Vocabulary is essential in order to achieve your desired IELTS band score. It vastly improves your written English and speaking skills, as well as your listening comprehension and grammar for the exam. "*IELTS 8.5.* **IELTS Vocabulary Masterclass**" is packed full of IELTS vocabulary, including phrasal verbs exercises and explanations. "*IELTS 8.5: IELTS Vocabulary Masterclass. Phrasal Verbs, Essay Vocabulary, Graph Vocabulary & Speaking Vocabulary*" is the best-selling new IELTS vocabulary book by Marc Roche, containing essential IELTS vocabulary, an IELTS phrasal verbs dictionary, vocabulary exercises for IELTS and IELTS speaking vocabulary.

"*IELTS 8.5: IELTS Vocabulary Masterclass. Phrasal Verbs, Essay Vocabulary, Graph Vocabulary & Speaking Vocabulary*" is ideal for anyone who has problems understanding, remembering and using vocabulary for the IELTS test and for anyone who wants to speak English fluently and confidently. Don´t waste hours upon hours researching vocabulary and trying to understand its meaning. This book will make your learning more efficient with less of your own effort, which means more spare time to review other concepts.

WHY YOU SHOULD READ THIS IELTS BOOK

IELTS 8.5: IELTS Vocabulary Masterclass. Phrasal Verbs, Essay Vocabulary, Graph Vocabulary & Speaking Vocabulary will give you the skills, tools, knowledge and practice needed to feel confident when tackling questions in all parts of the IELTS exam, and when speaking and understanding in English. This IELTS vocabulary book is a self-study step-by-step manual on how to use and understand IELTS terminology. Knowing this vocabulary will help prepare you for all the types of questions that you might have to answer in the exam.

The vocabulary included is essential for:

IELTS General

IELTS academic vocabulary

CHAPTER 1. IELTS VOCABULARY FOR GRAPH DESCRIPTIONS (IELTS ACADEMIC)

When you write a graph description for IELTS Academic Task 1, you will need to use language to describe changes, comparisons and contrasts.

We'll first focus on expanding your range of vocabulary and grammar structures for describing changes which can take place in a graph.

Exercise 1

Connect the vocabulary of change with the parts of the graph. More than one option is possible in some cases.

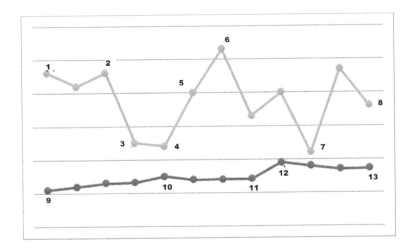

increased *steadily* or grew *steadily*	*Rose dramatically* or *increased dramatically*	
Plummeted to or *Plunged to* ...	*Hit a peak of,* or *Peaked at,* or *reached a high of* ...	*Fluctuated, varied,* or *oscillated. Became erratic*
Dropped/ Shrank/Fell drastically/ sharply dramatically	*Remained flat/unchanged/stable / constant at*	*Dropped and then stabilized/ evened out at*
Hit a low of .../ bottomed out at	*Dropped and then quickly recovered*	*Dipped / Declined slightly before quickly recovering*
Rocketed to / Soared to	*Fell slowly/ gradually / steadily*	*Was erratic/ inconsistent*

1-2 ....…

2-3 ....…

2-4 ....

4-6 ....

6 ....

6-8 ....

7 ....…

9-10 ....…

10-11 ....…

12-13 ....…

Definitions for some difficult words

Word	Explanation
Dipped	Fell slightly but recovered quickly
Bottomed out / Hit a low of	The lowest point on the graph
Plummeted to.../ Plunged to	Suffered a quick and drastic or shocking decrease. Fell extremely quickly. A very quick and large drop or reduction
Fluctuated/ was erratic	Increases and decreases randomly, irregularly or unpredictably
Rose/increased dramatically/ Soared/ Rocketed	Increased very quickly and drastically
Peaked at / reached a high of	The highest point on the graph
Remained constant/unchanged/stable at ..../ Levelled off/evened out at ...	a part of the graph where there is no change

Answers

1-2 Fell and then quickly recovered / Dipped/ fell slightly

2-3 Fell/dropped/shrank drastically/ dramatically / sharply/ Plummeted to/Plunged to

2-4 Dropped and then levelled off/evened out at

4-6 Rose/increased dramatically/Soared/ Rocketed

6 Hit a peak / Peaked at/reached a high of

6-8 Fluctuated/ was erratic

7 Hit a low of ...

9-10 Rose/increased steadily/ Rose/increased gradually

10-11 Remained flat/constant/unchanged/stable at

12-13 Fell gradually / steadily

CHAPTER 2. IELTS VOCABULARY FOR BAR CHARTS (IELTS ACADEMIC)

Bar Chart Language

To write a solid answer for task 1 in the Academic exam, you need to present the connections between the different parts of the chart or graph. You can do this by contrasting and comparing the information presented where necessary.

In most cases, you will not be using language of change to describe bar charts, instead you will be comparing and contrasting the information.

	Example	Comparative	Superlative
1 Syllable	High/Low/ Cold/Wet	Higher/Lower/Colder/Wetter	The highest/lowest/ coldest/wettest
3 or more syllables	Effective/ Popular	More Effective/ Popular	The most effective/ popular
Ending in -y	Healthy/Early	Healthier/Earlier	The healthiest/ earliest
Irregular adjectives	Bad/ Little (for quantity)	Worse/ Less	The worst/ least

2 Important Grammar Rules for this part:

1. Comparatives are made with *more* or *-er*, but NEVER both.

*The weather is getting **warmer**. (NOT ... more warmer.)*

*The game is getting **more popular**. (NOT ... more popularer.)*

2. Use superlatives to compare people and things with the groups or categories that they belong to.

Mary is the tallest of the five girls. (NOT Mary is the taller of the five girls.)

James is the oldest person in the class.

Other Important Language

Comparatives and superlatives are essential, but you can't over-rely on them.

Transitions

1. The UK imports close to 40 million tonnes of chocolate per year, <u>but</u> it produces only (a mere) 2% of the chocolate sold in Europe.

2. Spain produces large amounts of olive oil. <u>In comparison</u>, Italy produces very little.

3. China consumes more than a quarter of the world's meat. <u>On the other hand</u>, Germany consumes just 1.2% each year.

Subordinating Conjunctions

whether/ as much as/ once/ whereas/ that/ which/ whichever/ after/ as soon as/ as long as/ before/ by the time/ whom/ now that/ since/ till/ until/ when/ whenever/ while/ than/ though/ although /who/ whoever/ rather than/ whatever/ even though

1. China consumes more than a quarter of the world's meat, <u>while/whereas</u> Germany consumes just 1.2% each year.

2. While Germany consumes nearly 80 million tonnes of rice per year, it produces none.

3. Though Italy produced over 6 million tonnes of olives, Spain produced almost double during the same period.

Here are some structures for discussing similarities:

India consumes almost 100 million tonnes of rice per year; Likewise/ Similarly, China consumes 118.8 million.

Austria produced the same amount of butter as Switzerland in 2019.

Like Thailand, Malaysia produces 30,000 bottles.

Both the UK and Spain produce medium levels of carbon emissions.

Chapter 3. IELTS Vocabulary for Pie Charts (IELTS Academic)

You must demonstrate a variety of language in the IELTS Academic Writing exam. When describing pie charts, a variety of fractions and percentages are good. You should also use phrases to show when a number is not exact. Language like 'roughly', 'just under' or 'just over' are great in this type of description.

Here are some language examples to increase your flexibility when describing pie charts:

Percentages & Fractions

5% / one in twenty

10% / one in ten

15% / under one fifth (to express that this figure is small)

15% / almost one fifth (to express that this figure is large)

20% / one fifth

25% / one quarter

30% / under one third (to express that this figure is small)

30% / nearly one third (to express that this figure is large)

35% / over one third

40% / two-fifths

45% / over two fifths

50% / half

55% / over half

60% / three-fifths

65% / two-thirds

70% / seven in ten

75% / three-quarters

80% / four-fifths

Mini Exercise

Choose a qualifier from the list below and use it with a fraction to express the percentage on the left. The first one has been done for you as an example. You won't need to use all the options.

just over/just under/ almost / approximately/ nearly/ over

Percentage = Qualifier + Fraction

74% =   *nearly three-quarters*

48% =

15.5% =

63% =

69% =

Answers

Percentage = Qualifier + Fraction

48% =   just under half/ almost half

15.5% =approximately one fifth

15.5% =approximately one fifth

63% =   over three-fifths / almost two thirds

69% =   almost seven in ten

Exercise:

Pie Charts which Compare Past and Future

Use the lists of words 1-4 below to write your own sentences to describe a pie chart. Add the relevant data in brackets and change the verb tenses accordingly.

1. Diesel cars/account for (32%)/ traffic volume/ in 2019/ but/ in 2030/ forecast/represent (1%).

2. Estimate/success/rate/2021/(16%)/in contrast/to (29%)/2020.

3. in/ 2019/ smartphones/ make up/ bulk/ devices/ (82%) used/ but/ 2031/ this forecast/ drop to (30%)

1. ....
   ....

2. ....
   ....

3. ....
   ....

Answers:

1. Diesel cars accounted for 32% of traffic volume in 2019, but in 2030 they are forecast to represent 1%.

2. It is estimated that return on investment will fall to 16% in 2021 in contrast to 29% in 2020.

3. In 2019 smartphones made up the bulk of devices used (82%), but by 2031, this is forecast to drop to 30%.

CHAPTER 4. IELTS VOCABULARY FOR TABLES (IELTS ACADEMIC)

3 Important Points

1. You don't need to learn any new language to successfully describe a table in the IELTS exam.

2. When you start the task, you need to look for data that you can group together, as you would do in any other description.

3. Always start with the most interesting information (often the biggest things) and leave the least interesting data until the end of the description.

Exercise 1

Re-write sentences a-i using the language in the box below. You can make any necessary changes. There are four extra expressions you won't need to use.

> *The bulk of*
>
> *the lowest percentages*
>
> *was noticeably higher*
>
> *a smaller proportion of*
>
> *was significantly higher*
>
> *had the lowest percentages*
>
> *had slightly higher figures*
>
> *a third of the number of*
>
> *40% of*
>
> *Over 75%*
>
> *Three times the number of*
>
> *the largest proportion of*
>
> *One in four*

a. The Oasis concert was attended by three times as many people as the Blur concert.

b. More than four out of ten people chose to use trains.

c. The largest proportion of purchases came from Germany as opposed to the Spain.

d. A quarter of customers ordered print rather than digital products.

e. The website lost just under three quarters of its visitors when compared to last year.

f. Consumers in all countries spent more on toys than on any other product category.

g. Consumers spent the least on leisure/education in all countries.

h. Consumers in Turkey and Ireland spent quite a lot more on food, drinks and tobacco than consumers in the other countries.

i. Spending on clothing and footwear was a lot higher in Portugal, at 10%, than in the rest of the countries.

a. ....
....

b. ....
....

c. ....
....

d. ....
....

e. ....
....

f. ....
....

g. ....
....

h. ....
....

i. ....
....

Suggested Answers;

a. The Oasis concert was attended by **three times the number of** people of the Blur concert.

b. More than **40% of** people chose to use trains.

c. **The bulk of** purchases came from Germany as opposed to Spain.

d. **One in four** customers ordered print rather than digital products.

e. The social media website lost just **under 75%** of its visitors when compared to last year.

f. **The largest proportion** of spending in all countries was on toys.

g. The leisure/education category has **the lowest percentages** in the table.

h. Consumer spending on food, drinks and tobacco **was noticeably higher** in Turkey and Ireland than in the other countries.

i. Spending on clothing and footwear **was significantly higher** in Portugal, at 10%, than in the rest of the countries.

CHAPTER 5. IELTS VOCABULARY FOR PROCESSES (IELTS ACADEMIC)

Describing Sequences

The following linking words and phrases in the box **can** be used to describe a sequence.

before / prior to	At first / firstly/ initially
following that/ after that / next / then/ when	as soon as/ once / immediately after/ in turn
before	after
where	At the same time- simultaneously
finally	

Exercise 1:

Highlight or underline the linking words in A-G and decide which one is the first step in the sequence. Once you have done this, decide what is being described and put the sentences in order.

A. If it's being refurbished, the faulty components of the device are repaired in the factory

B. and the tablet is then returned to the shop as a refurbished product.

C. Once the device breaks, it is either discarded or refurbished.

D. They are then assembled at a different factory

E. First, the computer processors for the tablets are manufactured in an outsourced factory.

F. Then they are sent to the central warehouse for distribution around the country

G. Simultaneously, the exterior and the memory chip are produced.

Exercise 2:

Match 1 to 6 below with a sentence or phrase A-F to complete sequence descriptions. Please note that each full sentence belongs to a different description.

1. As soon as the bricks have been formed

2. After fermentation,

3. Once the oranges are ripe they are collected,

4. The water then flows into the penstock, which is a narrow chamber,

5. When the plant reaches a certain width, the leaves are picked.

6. In the early stages of milk production, cows graze in the field and subsequently (then-afterwards) taken to a milking machine twice a day.

A. the chocolate is placed into molds and left to cool down.

B. The raw product is then heated to a high temperature to kill bacteria and make it safe for human consumption. Following this, it is put into refrigeration storage.

C. and they are then spread (laid) out on a large (industrial sized) tray to enable them to dry under the sun.

D. they are left to dry.

E. they are then dried, sorted, blended and packaged ready for distribution to retailers.

F. and increases the pressure until the turbine turns.

Answers:

Exercise 1

Linking words: if, and , then, once, then, first, simultaneously.

The lifecycle of a tablet computer is being described.

E, G, D, F, C, A, B

Exercise 2

1d, 2a, 3c, 4f, 5e, 6b

Some Essential Vocabulary for Processes

Noun	Verb
Storage	Store
Pasteurization	Pasteurize
Harvest – harvesting	Harvest
Delivery	Deliver
Assembly	Assemble
Packing -Packaging	Pack - Package

Exercise 3:

Read the process description on the next page and fill in the blanks with the missing word or phrase.

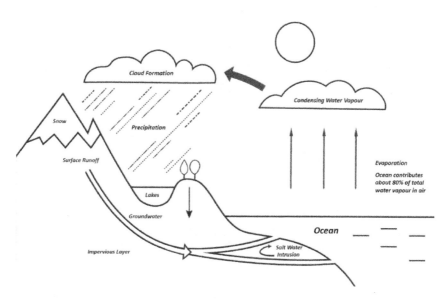

Diagram adapted from Nasa
https://gpm.nasa.gov/education/water-cycle

The diagram .... the water cycle. Firstly, water .... from the sea and floats into the atmosphere, ... **(two words)** accumulates in clouds and cools and condenses into rain or snow. The next stage shows the water's journey after falling to the ground, ... ends with .... **(three words)**

In the first stage of the ...., water, approximately 80% of which comes from Oceans, ... into the air as a result of the heat of the sun. After ...., the water vapor condenses to form clouds. An .... 80% of the water vapor comes from Oceans.

In the next ...., as clouds accumulate condensation they produce precipitation in the form of rain and snow. A large part of the water from the precipitation falls into lakes or is .... by the ground.

Part of the groundwater then .... back to the ocean without reaching the impervious layer through surface runoff.

................., Ocean water seeps through to the freshwater aquifers during the process is saltwater intrusion.

Answers:

The diagram **illustrates** the water cycle. Firstly, water **evaporates** from the sea and floats into the atmosphere, **where it** accumulates in clouds and cools and condenses into rain or snow. The next stage shows the water's journey after falling to the ground, **which** ends with **salt water intrusion**.

In the first stage of the **process**, water, approximately 80% of which comes from Oceans, **evaporates** into the air as a result of the heat of the sun. After **this**, the water vapor condenses to form clouds. An **estimated** 80% of the water vapor comes from Oceans.

In the next **stage**, as clouds accumulate condensation they produce precipitation in the form of rain and snow. A large part of the water from the precipitation falls into lakes or is **absorbed** by the ground.

Part of the groundwater then **flows** back to the ocean without reaching the impervious layer through surface runoff.

Finally, Ocean water seeps through to the freshwater aquifers during the process is saltwater intrusion.

CHAPTER 6. IELTS VOCABULARY FOR MAPS (IELTS ACADEMIC)

Verbs to describe changes in maps

Exercise 1

Match each beginning of a sentence 1-7 with an ending A-G. More than one option may be possible.

Notice the verb phrases underlined in A-G (we will look at these later).

1. The center of the village

2. Several old houses

3. A new hospital

4. The old factories

5. Some old mills

6. Some of the trees around the old park

7. The fire station

A. <u>replaced</u> the old run-down sports center *

B. <u>were knocked down</u> <u>to make way for</u> a new park.

C. <u>were pulled down</u>, with a new hotel <u>taking their place</u>

D. <u>were demolished</u> <u>to create</u> more space which <u>was turned into</u> a campsite

E. <u>were chopped down</u> in order <u>to increase the size of</u> path.

F. <u>was converted into</u> a gym and the car park <u>torn down</u>.

G. <u>was totally transformed</u> over the fifteen-year period.

* run-down is an adjective which means decaying, dirty old and not taken care of

Useful change phrases for map descriptions:

Replaced	took the place of
were knocked down to make way for	when a building or wall is deliberately destroyed to create space for something else
were pulled down	building or wall was destroyed especially because it was very old or dangerous
were demolished to create	when a building or wall is deliberately destroyed to create space for something else
was turned into	were transformed or changed into something else
were chopped down	the action of cutting trees until they fall
to increase the size of	generic term for: to make bigger or wider
to reduce the size of	generic term for: to make smaller or narrower
taking their place	occupying the place where the other thing used to be
was converted into	was transformed or changed into
was torn down	was knocked down

Exercise 2

Underline the most appropriate verb in bold in sentences 1-8 and put it into the right form to suit the sentence.

1. The abandoned car-park near the woodlands **develop/become** into a museum.

2. The area around the city center **turn into/become** less accessible with the construction of the new theatre.

3. As the city **extend/expand**, more bus stations were built.

4. A bus station **construct/ become** after the old warehouses were knocked down.

5. The downtown area of the city completely **change/demolish** with the introduction of the new shopping center.

6. A number of important developments **take place/ convert**, which totally **alter/expand** the character of the premises.

7. The area **turn into/become** more family-friendly with the **introduce/ knock down** of new parks and open spaces.

8. The road was **extend/expand** to the town center, and a new bus service was introduced to carry passengers to and from the airport.

....
....

....
....

....
....

....
....

....
....

....
....

....
....

....
....

....
....

....
....

The two maps below show an island, before and after the construction of some tourist facilities.

Summarise the information by selecting and reporting the main features, and make comparisons where relevant.

Write at least 150 words.

Before

Sea

Sea

Beach

100 Metres

After

Sea

Swimming

Beach

Restaurant

Reception

Accommodation

Pier

100 Metres

Footpath
Vehicle track

Image Source: Cambridge English Practice Tests.
https://www.cambridge.org/gb/cambridgeenglish/catalog/cambridge-english-exams-ielts/resources

Exercise 3:

Look at the following map task from an IELTS test. Read the sample answer on the next page and fill in the blanks with the missing word or phrase.

The two maps below show an island, before and after the construction of some tourist facilities.

Summarise the information by selecting and reporting the main features, and make comparisons where relevant.

Write at least 150 words.

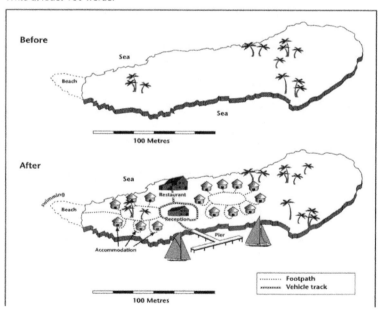

Image Source: Cambridge English Practice Tests.
https://www.cambridge.org/gb/cambridgeenglish/catalog/cambridge-english-exams-ielts/resources

Sample Description:

The two maps illustrate the changes which have .... **(two words)** on a small island, prior to and after its development for tourism.

The introduction of tourism on the island has .... **(two words)** the landscape, with several new developments that can be seen in the second diagram. The most important changes are that the island now has ample accommodation for tourists and there is a peer to enable visitors to access the island.

One of the most striking changes are the accommodation huts which are connected by footpaths and which have been .... around the reception and restaurant area. A total of 6 huts, have been constructed in the west of the island and another 9 have been built around the center of the island.

A pier has also been developed on the south coast of the island to make the island .... to tourists and there is a short road linking it with the reception and restaurant. The trees which were scattered around the island have been left untouched, and a swimming area has been .... just off the beach.

Answers:

Exercise 1

1. G
2. B/C/D
3. A
4. B/C/D
5. B/C/D
6. E
7. A/F

Exercise 2

1. developed / was developed
2. became
3. expanded
4. was constructed
5. was completely changed / completely changed
6. took place, altered
7. became , introduction
8. was extended

Exercise 3

The two maps illustrate the changes which have taken place on a small island, prior to and after its development for tourism.

The introduction of tourism on the island has significantly changed the landscape, with several new developments that can be seen in the second diagram. The most important changes are that the island now has ample accommodation for tourists and there is a peer to enable visitors to access the island.

One of the most striking changes are the accommodation huts which are connected by footpaths and which have been built around the reception and restaurant area. A total of 6 huts, have been constructed in the west of the island and another 9 have been built around the center of the island.

A pier has also been developed on the south coast of the island to make the island accessible to tourists and there is a short road linking it with the reception and restaurant. The trees which were scattered around the island have been left untouched, and a swimming area has been designated just off the beach.

Chapter 7. IELTS Vocabulary for Essays (IELTS Academic IELTS General Training)

Connecting words and set phrases

Putting your reasons in order	Firstly/Secondly. Thirdly/Finally
Expressing an opinion	I hold the view that ... In my view... It is probably true to say that.... There can be no doubt that ...
Mentioning what other people think	It has been suggested that.... There are those who believe that.. There are those who argue that... Opponents/ supporters of (e.g. hunting) ... argue that.... Most people hold firmly to the belief that... It is often claimed that...
Common opinions in society	It is widely believed/thought that Few people would contest

	that.... Nobody would dispute the fact that .... It is generally agreed that...
Referring to evidence and facts	Research suggests that... All the evidence suggests that ... Recent evidence indicates that .....
Changing direction	However/Nevertheless
Giving examples	For example for instance such as
Concluding	In conclusion / Overall,

Exercise 1

Fill the gaps with an appropriate word or phrase from the box:

To conclude	I hold the view that	however.	Firstly, research suggests that
may	which can lead to	For instance,	when people
they are more likely to	Secondly, few people would contest that	Therefore	it is likely that
Finally,	such as	However, there are those who argue that	nobody would contest the fact that
In addition, it is often claimed that	Nobody would dispute the fact that	there can be no doubt that	Hence,

Model Essay

.... many programs on television include violent scenes, especially action and horror movies. .... they should not be allowed, ... many people disagree with this opinion. In this essay, I will discuss both sides and give reasons for my opinion.

........., ... people who watch violent programs and play violent computer games .... worry more about their own safety,

.... problems in society. ...., ... are worried about their safety, ... react aggressively towards strangers.
.... some children copy what they see on television and in computer games. ...... if they are watching and interacting with violence on a daily basis .... they will copy this type

of behavior. ...., there are more beneficial activities that children could be participating in, ... playing a sport or reading a book.

.... violence is not something we learn from television and computer games. For example, ... there were murders before television and videogames were invented. ....,

.... children cannot watch violent programs and play inappropriate videogames easily. For instance, there are restrictions for some programmes and games, and many parents do not allow their children to watch television after a certain time.

.... , although there are some reasonable arguments against higher restrictions on violent videogames and programmes for children, ... the potential disadvantages of children copying what they see and hear in these programmes and games far outweigh the advantages of having free access to them. Furthermore, current restrictions are ineffective and easy to ignore. .... , governments and local institutions should do more to promote alternative activities and to engage young people in their local communities from an early age.

Answers:

Nobody would dispute the fact that many programs on television include violent scenes, especially action and horror movies. **I hold the view that** they should not be allowed, **however** many people disagree with this opinion. In this essay, I will discuss both sides and give reasons for my opinion.

Firstly, **research suggests that** people who watch violent programs and play violent computer games **may** worry more about their own safety, **which can lead to** problems in society. **For instance**, **when people** are worried about their safety, **they are more likely to** react aggressively towards strangers. **Secondly**, **few people would contest that** some children copy what they see on television and in computer games. **Hence**, if they are watching and interacting with violence on a daily basis **it is likely that** they will copy this type of behavior. **Finally**, there are more beneficial activities that children could be participating in **such as** playing a sport or reading a book.

However, there are those who argue that violence is not something we learn from television and computer games. For example, **nobody would contest the fact that** there were murders before television and videogames were invented. **In addition**, **it is often claimed that** children cannot watch violent programs and play inappropriate videogames easily. For instance, there are restrictions for some programmes and games, and many parents do not allow their children to watch television after a certain time.

To conclude, although there are some reasonable arguments against higher restrictions on violent videogames and programmes for children, **there can be no doubt that** the potential disadvantages of children copying what they see and hear in these programmes and games far outweigh the advantages of having free access to them. Furthermore, current restrictions are ineffective and easy to ignore. **Therefore**, governments and local institutions should do more to promote alternative activities and to engage young people in their local communities from an early age.

The words in the box below are all useful examples of words like 'argument', which you can use with the word 'this' (or 'these' in plural) to specify more information.

analysis	approach	concept	context
data	definition	environment	evidence
factor	issue	problem	function
measure	method	period	policy
principle	procedure	process	theory
response	sector	structure	interpretation

Here is an example of how we can use this structure in an essay.

There is no doubt that corruption is the most important point to focus on, because it originates from positions of power. Corruption can take many shapes and forms, such as political, which involves crimes in a country's legal system and within the police, and economic, for example by misusing tax money. All the evidence suggests that countries with corrupt governments are not able to develop as fast as countries where there is less corruption.

These factors [...].

OR

This negative environment [...].

The first sentence of a paragraph is vital, as it shows how it connects with the overall structure, and can signal what will happen next.

When you practice writing, always check that your essay is logical by underlining the most important sentences in each paragraph. You should be able to understand the whole essay only by reading those sentences. If you can't, you need to make changes.

Chapter 8. IELTS Vocabulary for Letters & Emails (IELTS General Training)

8.1 LETTER OF REFERENCE

In this type of formal letter, you're asked to provide a reference for a colleague or friend to a prospective employer or educational institution.

You may find it helpful to note down useful expressions which you can include,

Some Useful Language for this type of letter or email

I have known X for ....

I am confident that ....

I have no hesitation in recommending him ....

X is sociable, reliable, self-confident, outgoing

X possesses a thorough grounding in ...

stand him in good stead

as is shown by the fact that ...

Exercise 1:

Look at the gaps in sample answer below:

Where could you use these linking words and discourse markers to complete the text? You will not need to sue all of them.

Firstly, in addition, for instance, moreover, furthermore or by way of example.

Sample Answer (Letter of Reference):

To whom it may concern,

Mary and I worked together at J&J Retail for 10 years.

It is my pleasure to recommend her for the position of shop assistant.

1......................, Mary is a self-confident and outgoing person, who finds it easy to relate to people from all kinds of backgrounds.

During her time at J&J Retail, Mary proved to be friendly, communicative, hard-working and excellent at managing her time. 2....................., Mary is the kind of person who works well with others, as she displays great sensitivity and sympathy. She was always willing to contribute and help her colleagues. 3.................... at J&J Retail she was popular and fully committed to the organisation's objectives.

4.................... at J&J Retail, Mary demonstrated excellent English language skills dealing with English-speaking customers on a daily basis. She passed her English exams around 6 months ago and has a keen interest in fashion, which I am sure will stand her in good stead when she is helping customers in English.

I recommend Mary without reservation — she would be an excellent asset to your company.

Please do not hesitate to contact me if you have any questions.

Sincerely,

Now you can check your answers by reading "Sample Answer (Letter of Reference)" on the next page...

Sample Answer (Letter of Reference):

To whom it may concern,

Mary and I worked together at J&J Retail for 10 years.

It is my pleasure to recommend her for the position of shop assistant.

Firstly, Mary is a self-confident and outgoing person, who finds it easy to relate to people from all kinds of backgrounds.

During her time at J&J Retail, Mary proved to be friendly, communicative, hard-working and excellent at managing her time. In addition, Mary is the kind of person who works well with others, as she displays great sensitivity and sympathy. She was always willing to contribute and help her colleagues. Moreover, (Furthermore) at J&J Retail she was popular and fully committed to the organisation's objectives.

By way of example, (For instance) at J&J Retail, Mary demonstrated excellent English language skills dealing with English-speaking customers on a daily basis. She passed her English exams around 6 months ago and has a keen interest in fashion, which I am sure will stand her in good stead when she is helping customers in English.

I recommend Mary without reservation — she would be an excellent asset to your company.

Please do not hesitate to contact me if you have any questions.

Sincerely,

Your name and Surname

(Word count: 197)

Reference pronouns:

Reference pronouns like *this, that, they* or *it* are commonly used to refer back to something or someone recently mentioned.

Relative clauses:

Relative clauses can be used to give added information to a statement and they allow you to link ideas together in well-formed sentences.

Substitution:

Other forms of cohesive devices include things like substitution. This is where you use a synonym for example to refer backwards or forwards to a connected point in the text.

E.g. Replacing a verb phrase:

The management team at J & J Retails were very happy with Mary, and so were the rest of the staff (and the rest of the staff were also very happy with her).

Using paragraphs and a variety of cohesive devices effectively will help you score well in the "Coherence and Cohesion" and "Task achievement" parts of the assessment criteria. **Tip:** When you're reading, make a point of looking out for cohesive devices like the ones we've looked at in this section.

8.2 LETTER OF COMPLAINT:

I am writing to complain about...

I would like to express my dissatisfaction with ...

I am writing to express my concern about the....

I must complain in writing about...

I feel I must complain to you about...

I wish to complain in the strongest terms about...

I am writing to inform you of an apparent error in your records...

Paraphrasing exercise:

Example:

0) Basic Problem: *"I want to complain about the bad service in the restaurant. "*

ii. Key Language: *I would like to express my dissatisfaction with ...*

iii, Key Word you must use: POOR (Bad is too informal, so we can use *poor* instead)

iv. Final Product: *"I would like to express my dissatisfaction with the poor standard of service in the restaurant. "*

Now try to complete the process using the following language:

1)

i. Basic problem: *"The cinema is really far away from everything"*

ii. Key Phrase: *I wish to complain in the strongest terms about...*

iii, Key Word: ACCESSIBILITY

iv. Final Product:

....

....

2)

i. Basic problem: *"During my course, there were too many students in the class"*

ii. Key Phrase: *I am writing to express my concern about the....*

iii, Key Word: NUMBER

iv. Final Product:

....

....

Answers:

1) I wish to complain in the strongest terms about the accessibility of the cinema.

2) I am writing to express my concern about the number of students in the class during my course

Topic specific phrases

• *Poor standard of service/slow service*

• *I am asking for/I would like to request a replacement*

• *No accommodation/Travel delays/Rather rude staff*

• *Badly scratched/dented wrapping/packaging*

• *To claim/demand for a refund*

• *I am returning ... to you for correction of the fault/for inspection/repair/servicing*

• *Defective/faulty goods/defective item/machine*

• *The... may need replacing*

• *To restore an item to full working order...*

• *I am enclosing the broken radio in this package; please send me a replacement..*

• *You said that ... I feel sure there must be some mistake as I am sure that...*

Ending the letter

• *I do not usually complain, but, as an old customer, I hope you will be interested in my comments.*

• *We look forward to dealing with this matter without delay.*

• I feel that your company should consider an appropriate refund.

• I would be grateful if you would send me a complete refund as soon as possible

•We feel there must be some explanation for (this delay) and expect your prompt reply.

• Will you please look into this matter and let us know the reason for ...

• Thank you for your assistance.

• I look forward to hearing from you at your earliest convenience.

• I am returning the damaged goods/items... and shall be glad if you will replace them.

• Please look into this matter at once and let me know the delay.

• Please check your records again.

• Thank you for your cooperation in correcting this detail...

• I wish to draw your attention to...

• I would suggest that...

• I suggest that immediate steps be taken.

• I wish to complain about...

- *I look forward to a prompt reply and hope that you will take into*

consideration...

- *I am really dissatisfied with...*

Now look at the sample answer for the question we looked at earlier in this section. Pay special attention to the language and structure used.

Sample Answer

Dear Sir/Madam,

I would like to express my dissatisfaction with the poor standard of service we received during our recent visit to Dino's Bar. Firstly, the staff were generally quite rude and unhelpful, they seemed to lack basic food knowledge and they did not seem interested in the job. For instance, none of them could offer any advice to me on choosing a dish.

A further cause for complaint was that the food was cold when it arrived to our table. I understand that it was a busy night, but, we booked the table and the menus the day before, so I feel that they should have been ready.

Finally, not only did we receive substandard food and unfriendly, unhelpful service, but we were also charged full price for our meals after we complained. In my opinion the prices seem to be very expensive for the quality of the food and the service provided.

I do not usually complain, but, as a loyal customer, I hope you will be interested in my comments. Perhaps it would be appropriate to offer some training courses to staff at Dino´s Bar, in order to avoid this from happening again. I feel that customer service was a big issue, as was the quality of the food. If these two problems were fixed, then price might not be such an issue in the future, as customers would be happy to pay little more for a better experience. I hope you will take these points into consideration

I look forward to your reply.

Yours faithfully,

Name and Surname

8.3 Formal Letters: Structure Rules

Greeting

Name unknown: *Dear Sir/Madam,*

Name known: *Dear Mr.../ Dear Mrs... / Dear Ms..+ surname*

Reason for writing

I am writing to ... I am writing with regard to ...

I am writing on behalf of ...

Asking questions

I would be grateful if ... I wonder if you could ....

Could you ...?

Referring to someone else's letter /points

As you stated in your letter, ...   Regarding .../ Concerning ...

With regard to ....

Finishing the letter

If you require any further information, please do not hesitate to contact me.

I look forward to hearing from you.

Signing

If Dear + name = Yours sincerely,

If Dear Sir/ Madam = Yours faithfully

Your first name + surname must be written clearly under your signature

8.4 Formal Letter IELTS General Exam Checklist.

When you have written your letter, check:

1. It is a formal letter

2. It includes all the information necessary

3. You have asked all the questions you need to

4. The questions are correctly formulated indirect questions

5. The letter is divided into paragraphs

6. You have checked the letter carefully for mistakes

Formal Letters: Language

Letters can be anything from very formal to very informal. The IELTS General Writing paper will never ask you to write a specialized business or legal letter requiring a professional knowledge of business words, structures and expressions. However, they might ask you to write a formal, a semi-formal or an informal email or letter.

In this section of the chapter, we will focus on your use of language and in particular, your ability to create a formal register. This will help you to do well in two of the assessment criteria: language of course in terms of using a range of formal vocabulary and grammatical structures and communicative achievement by being able to create an appropriate formal tone that has a positive effect on the reader. We will identify some of the features of formal English that we often find in formal letters.

At the end of this section you will find a list of useful formal-informal equivalents. This list will save you a lot of time in your preparation for the exam. For example, in a letter of complaint: *"I was rather disappointed"* is a formal way of

81

saying *"I was furious"* or *"I was very angry"*. See how many more formal and informal equivalent items you can learn next.

Exercise 1:

Transform the informal or semi-formal version of each phrase from a letter of complaint into a formal style. You can make small changes to the content of the sentences if you think it's necessary and you can use a dictionary.

Example: I thought I'd write = I am writing

a. state of the playground =
....

b. I have noticed loads of rubbish =
....

c. I reckon =
....

d. The teacher I'm talking about =
....

e. On top of this =

....

f. a load of problems =

....

g. You could =

....

h. stop = ...

i. What's more =

....

j. better = ...

k. To finish =

....

l. I'm looking forward to hearing from you =

....

83

Answers:

a. state of the playground = condition of the playground

b. I have noticed loads of rubbish = There is a great deal of litter

c. I reckon = It is my opinion that...

d. The teacher I'm talking about = The teacher in question OR The teacher I am referring to

e. On top of this = Furthermore

f. a load of problems = a number of problems

g. You could = it may be possible for you

h. stop = prevent

i. What's more = In addition

j. better = more suitable OR more adequate

k. To finish = In conclusion

l. I'm looking forward to hearing from you = I look forward to your reply OR I look forward to hearing from you

Exercise 2:

Now here are some full sentences from formal letters.
Complete the sentences using only one word.

a. I am writing in .... to your job advertisement in the
ABC newspaper

b. I would like to .... for the position of translator.

c. I am .... to come for interview at any time
convenient to you.

d. I would be .... if you could send me further
information regarding the position.

e. Please find my CV ....

f. I would like to express my .... with the poor standard
of service we received during our recent visit to your cinema.

g. For ...., none of them could offer any advice to me on choosing a dish.

h. Finally, not only .... we receive substandard food and unfriendly, unhelpful service, but we were also charged full price for our meals after we complained.

i. I look forward to your reply.

Answers:

a. I am writing in reply/response to your job advertisement in the ABC newspaper

b. I would like to apply for the position of translator.

c. I am available/ able to come for interview at any time convenient to you.

d. I would be grateful if you could send me further information regarding the position.

e. Please find my CV attached (email)/ enclosed (letter).

f. I would like to express my dissatisfaction with the poor standard of service we received during our recent visit to your cinema.

g. For instance, none of them could offer any advice to me on choosing a dish.

h. Finally, not only did we receive substandard food and unfriendly, unhelpful service, but we were also charged full price for our meals after we complained.

j.   *I look forward to your reply.*

Use of the Passive (Sometimes)

Okay, the next example is one where the passive has been used instead of an active form. This is a common feature of formal writing but should not be overused.

This sentence is an example of how we might structure a sentence formally.

Informal: *"The waiter did offer us another dish, but when it arrived it was cold again."*

Formal: *"Although we were offered an alternative dish, when it was delivered to the table it was cold again".*

Notice two clauses in the informal version are joined by but whereas in the formal version, the two clauses have been reversed and but is replaced with although which starts the sentence. This is a more formal way of saying the same thing.

Within the formal sentence *"Although we were offered an alternative dish, when it was delivered to the table it was cold again"*, there are further examples of vocabulary that is more formal than the equivalent in the informal version. For example, *alternative dish* is a more formal way of saying *another dish.*

As we saw above, phrasal verbs are most typical of informal letters —although there are some which have no more formal equivalents and are common in all types of letter (*look forward to,* for example). Most phrasal verbs, however, do have formal equivalents and these would be preferred in most formal letters whereas the formal equivalents would be very rarely used in an informal letter.

6 Quick Rules of Formal VS Informal:

1. We tend to understate our feelings and would say *I was rather disappointed* or *I was somewhat surprised* instead of saying how we really felt.

2. For the same reason, we do not use exclamation marks.

3. We often use the passive to emphasize the action when the person is of less importance

4. We avoid contractions in formal letters.

5. We use formal equivalence of idiomatic language and phrasal verbs

6. Particular sentence structures can be used to create a formal tone. Inversion is one example of this "Although we were offered an alternative dish, when it was delivered to the table it was cold again".

Exercise 3:

Rewrite the following sentences using formal equivalents for the phrasal verbs. Use a dictionary if necessary. You might need to make other changes to the structures.

1) I'm so chuffed that you've been talked into coming to the meeting.

....

....

2) The football club's facilities have been done up, so this should make our performances better.

....

....

3) As our town is quite cut off, perhaps we could arrange for you to be put up in a hotel in the city for a few days.

....

....

91

4) We will make up for the inconvenience of having to wait for so long.

....

....

Answers:

1) I am very happy that you have been convinced to attend the meeting.

2) The football club's facilities have been refurbished, which should improve our performances.

3) As our town is quite isolated, we could arrange hotel accommodation in the city for a few days.

4) We will compensate you for the inconvenience of having to wait for so long.

8.5 Informal Letters

The informal letter is going to be very friendly, very relaxed, very easy language.

LET'S START WITH A TYPICAL TASK.

An English-speaking friend is visiting your region for a couple of weeks during his holidays and has written to you to ask for several recommendations.

Write a letter to your friend.

In your letter you should:

• offer to help find accommodation

• give advice about things to do

• provide information about what clothes to bring..

In this type of task, you should begin your letter as follows:

Dear ... your friend's name.

A few things to keep in mind.

• You have about 20 minutes to write this.

• You should have at least 150 words. Aim for about 180 (a little bit more but don't go too long- If you're over 240 words, you've written much more than you need to.)

• Address the points, have your opening and closing and that's it!

Let's start with the general idea of what you're trying to do, what you're trying to accomplish.

The tone:

'The tone' of the letter means how your letter sounds, or the overall feeling it gives the reader. It should be very relaxed, very informal, this is what the examiners are looking for.

For example: if you're writing to your friend, write it as though you were speaking to your friend; very casual.

You can start with:

Dear- Hello- Hi and then the person's first name, never their surname.

You shouldn't use *Mr., Mrs., Dr..*

Do not put first and last name because you do not address your friend or family member by his or her first and last name in real life.

Use contractions:

Now contractions are suitable. So in terms of how you're going to use I've, it's, don't etc.., In a formal letter, you say do not whereas in an informal letter, you say don't.

Slang and idioms

Not only are slang and idioms okay now, they're actually recommended because they demonstrate that you can adapt your language to different contexts. When you speak with your friends, you normally use very casual language including slang and idioms.

Nevertheless, remember it has to be natural, so don't be too heavy on the slang or the idioms. One or two here and there are great, but if you overuse them, it becomes unnatural and the examiners may penalise you for it.

Note that you can use idioms in your formal letter as well but very carefully, very selectively and it has to be very appropriate, so it's generally not recommended.

Stay organized and focused:

You still have to remember what it is you're doing and make it very clear in the letter. Are you thanking the person, are you answering a question, are you asking for something, are you offering advice? Make this clear right away in the introduction. Make sure the body follows.

Language

Again, you don't want to use very serious language in an informal letter or email, you don't want to use too many formal or complex words because that's not how we speak to friends and family normally.

With our friends we're usually very casual and relaxed.

For example:

I just wanted to say thanks for helping me out last week.

In a formal letter, you would write

I'm writing to express my appreciation and gratitude for your assistance with last week's matter..

Notice the different feel of the two sentences. One is very casual, one is very formal.

Another example:

Should you require any further information, please do not hesitate to contact me - formal.

<u>Versus</u>

Let me know if you need anything else - super casual.

To make your letter look real, the best thing you can do is ALWAYS rely on your personal experience.

Formal VS Informal Language List:

It is vital that you can distinguish between formal and informal language in English, not only for this exam, but also for communication in general. Writing a letter or email to a friend is obviously not the same as writing a letter of recommendation for a friend who has applied for a job. Here are some examples of formal and informal words with the same meaning,

VERBS:

FORMAL: INFORMAL

to depart: to go

to carry out: to do

to provide: to give

to retain: keep

to cease: stop

to seek: look for

assist, aid: to help

liberate: to free

obtain: to get

to desire: want

request: to ask for

to function: work

to demonstrate: show

to reside: live

require: need

OTHER WORDS:

FORMAL: INFORMAL

subsequently: next / later

immature, infantile: childish

sufficient: enough

further: more (information)

hence, therefore: so

deficiency, lack of: little, there is no

perspiration: sweat

inexpensive: cheap

Chapter 9. Important Phrasal Verbs for IELTS

What is a phrasal verb?

Phrasal verbs are a group of two or more words which perform the same function as another verb. A phrasal verb is a phrase that is made up of a main verb and an adverb, a preposition or both. They are idiomatic ways of expressing an action. Think of it like a sandwich:

[Main Verb] + adverb/preposition/adverb and preposition = phrasal verb

Phrasal verbs are unique to English and other Germanic languages and can cause issues for English learners. They can be transitive (they take a direct object), intransitive (they do not take a direct object), separable (they can be separated) and inseparable (they cannot be separated). We will cover the differences between these, complete with descriptions and exercises, later on.

Although the meanings differ, phrasal verbs are conjugated just like main verbs. For example, to break down conjugates like to break:

The car breaks down.

The car broke down.

Here are some common phrasal verbs to get you started:

Phrasal Verb   bring up

Example *He brought up the fact that I was too short to go on the rollercoaster.*

Meaning: to mention a topic

Phrasal Verb   call off

Example *She called off the wedding.*

Meaning: to cancel

Phrasal Verb   carry on

Example *The bag was heavy and my feet hurt, but I carried on with the walk.*

Meaning: to continue

Phrasal Verb   deal with

Example *I can't deal with stress.*

Meaning: to handle

Phrasal Verb   end up

Example *They ended up in Sheffield.*

Meaning: to reach a state or place

Phrasal Verb   fall through

Example *Our plans to meet for coffee fell through.*

Meaning: to not happen

Phrasal Verb   get on with (something)

Example *She was busy, so I got on with my essay.*

Meaning: to continue to do

Phrasal Verb   hand in

Example *I handed in my thesis.*

Meaning: to submit

Phrasal Verb   join in

Example *She joined in the conversation at the party.*

Meaning: to participate

Phrasal Verb   keep up with

Example *My boss talks too fast and I can't keep up.*

Meaning: to stay at the same pace or level.

Phrasal Verb   let down

Example *She was supposed to collect me at 6:00 but she didn't. She really let me down.*

Meaning: to disappoint

Phrasal Verb   look forward to

Example *Are you looking forward to your holiday?*

Meaning: to be excited about something, to anticipate something good.

Phrasal Verb   mix up

Example *I can't tell the twins apart; I always mix up their names.*

Meaning: to mistake one thing for another

Phrasal Verb   pass away

Example *My grandfather passed away last night.*

Meaning: to die

Phrasal Verb   put off

Example *I kept putting it off, even though I knew I had to do it*

Meaning: to postpone

Phrasal Verb   rule out

Example *We know it wasn't John who ate Sarah's pasta, so we can rule him out*

Meaning: to eliminate

Phrasal Verb   stick up for (someone)

Example *Catherine was always getting bullied, so Alex stuck up for her.*

Meaning: to defend

Phrasal Verb   think over

Example *Janine told Roger that she would have to think over his proposal.*

Meaning: to consider

Phrasal Verb   work out

Example

1. *It's important for your fitness that you work out three times a week.*

2. *The Maths problem was difficult but I eventually worked it out.*

Meaning:

1. to do physical exercise

2. to solve a problem

Do phrasal verbs make any sense?

If you analyze them logically, no.. However, let's try to find some logic....

The meanings of phrasal verbs are not immediately obvious, for example:

Tom broke up with Jenny.

Tom separated from Jenny.

We know that Tom did not break Jenny into small pieces, he stopped being her boyfriend. This is an example of a phrasal verb not being directly linked to the meaning of its main verb.

However, sometimes with phrasal verbs we can work backwards to understand the logic of them. Breaking something does not have to be completely physical, it can also be figurative. The idea is that you are breaking a bond between someone. Because of this meaning, we can also use to break up to mean:

- Separate people from fighting: I had to break up a fight.

- A poor connection: I tried to call her but the line kept breaking up.

At first glance, you may not see a link between to break and to break up, but when you work backwards and think figuratively, the meaning becomes clearer.

How will I learn them?

As with any item of vocabulary, you will have to learn them individually. The more English media that you consume, the more phrasal verbs you will learn.

TASK 1

Try to match the phrasal verbs below with their synonyms:

Phrasal Verb *Example*

a. throw away *John threw away his apple core.*

b. look into *Sarah looked into the murder case.*

c. get away with *The robber got away with the crime.*

d. use up *Use up the washing-up liquid before you buy another bottle!*

e. run out of *My phone ran out of battery.*

Meanings:

1. use completely

2. exhaust supply

3. investigate

4. discard

5. escape blame

Check your answers at the bottom of the next page.

When can I use Phrasal Verbs?

Phrasal verbs are used in non-formal situations. You will hear them used in speech on a daily basis, in emails between friends, and in some magazines. They are becoming more and more prevalent, but there are certain situations where you should avoid using them:

- Formal letters or emails.

- Academic papers or presentations.

TASK 2:

In the following email, underline all the phrasal verbs that you can find and write their meanings below. You may need to use a dictionary.

Hi Jack,

I'm sorry that I was late to work today. My car broke down yesterday, so I took the bus instead. However, the bus was held up in traffic! It seems that everyone was going to work at the same time!

Don't worry about the project, I'll be able to catch up with the rest of my colleagues. I'll drop by the office on the weekend and see if there is anything extra that I can do.

I hope you've got over your cold, I hear it's been going round the office recently.

Best wishes,

Gary

(1)   /

(2)   /

(3)   /

(4)   /

(5)   /

(6)   /

ANSWERS

Task 1:

a) 4

b) 3

c) 5

d) 1

e) 2

Task 2:

(1) break down / to stop working

(2) hold up / to delay (to be held up- to be delayed)

(3) catch up / to do tasks

(4) drop by / visit briefly

(5) get over / to recover from an illness

(6) go round / to affect a lot of people

Chapter 10. Types of Phrasal Verb

There are 4 types of phrasal verb:

Transitive phrasal verbs

Intransitive phrasal verbs

Separable phrasal verbs

Inseparable phrasal verbs

Transitive and Intransitive Phrasal Verbs

There are two types of verbs in English: Transitive and Intransitive. Transitive verbs take a direct object, whereas intransitive verbs do not.

Transitive phrasal verbs

These phrasal verbs take a direct object:

I look after my sister on Mondays

I	*look after*	+	*my sister*	*on Mondays*
	[phrasal verb]	+	[direct object]	

Intransitive phrasal verbs

These phrasal verbs do not take a direct object:

When I grow up, I want to be a firefighter.

| When | I | grow up | I want to be a firefighter |
| | | [phrasal verb] | |

Task 1

Look at the phrasal verbs below in the table with their examples. Decide whether they are transitive or intransitive. (You can find the answers at the end of this section).

Phrasal Verb: Example

1. **Take out**   *Please take out the bins before you leave.*

2. **Cheer up**   *I need to cheer up my sister because she's crying.*

3. **Come back**   *I'm waiting for my mother to come back from the shops.*

4. **Go through**   *I went through my father's bottle of cologne.*

5. **Get up**   *I get up every morning at 6am.*

6. **Get by**   *It was a difficult year and Mrs Calloway lost her job, but they got by.*

7. **Pass out**   *She passed out because of the amount of pain she was suffering from.*

8. **Get along with**   *He gets along with most people.*

Task 2

Read the following sentences. They are all transitive. Underline the transitive verbs and highlight the direct object.

1. He is so creative; he made up a story for his daughter and her friends.

2. I have to fill out this form so I can go to university.

3. Can you help me hang up this picture?

4. There was a problem with his essay; he had left out a conclusion.

5. The old friends ran into each other on the street.

6. I don't like how she looks down on everyone.

7. We tried on the costumes but we looked awful in them!

8. She takes after her grandmother.

9. My mother says I have to get rid of my old toys.

10. I can't hear anything - please turn up the volume!

You can find the answers at the end of this section.

Separable and Inseparable Phrasal Verbs

As phrasal verbs consist of a main verb, an adverb or preposition or both, these verbs can sometimes be separated. Only transitive verbs (which take a direct object) can be separated.

Separable phrasal verbs

These phrasal verbs, as the name suggests, can be separated:

Turn off the light before you leave.

Turn the light off before you leave.

Only transitive phrasal verbs (which take a direct object) can be separated. However, it is important to remember:

All separable phrasal verbs are transitive, but not all transitive phrasal verbs are separable.

Turn off	+	*the light*	*before you leave.*
[Phrasal verb]	+	[direct object]	

115

Turn + *the light* + *off before you leave.*

[PV part 1] + [direct object] + [PV part 2]

Inseparable phrasal verbs

These phrasal verbs, as the name suggests, can't be separated:

He passed away last night.

He   passed away   last night

      [inseparable verbs]

They cannot be separated due to the fact that there is no direct object. The phrase *'last night'* is an adverb.

Word Order

When separating phrasal verbs, there is a word order that must be adhered to:

When referring to a specific object or person, the object can go between the phrasal verb or after the phrasal verb:

I picked up Sophie from school.

I picked Sophie up from school.

116

When using a pronoun as the direct object, the pronoun can only go between the phrasal verb:

I picked her up from school.

Task 3

The following phrases are separable phrasal verbs. **Write out the different ways to separate the phrasal verb using correct word order.**

Example:

I hung up the picture on the wall.

I hung the picture up on the wall.

I hung it up on the wall.

1. She put out the fire.

....

....

....

....

2.   I called off the party.

....

....

....

....

3.   Oscar asked out Samantha.

....

....

....

....

4.   They handed in their essays on time.

....

....

....

....

5.   I like showing off my new boots.

....

....

....

....

6.   Turn off the washing machine!

....

....

....

....

7.   I have to drop off my sister at a party.

....

....

....

....

8.   She won't give up her love of singing.

....

....

....

....

9.   Put on your hat.

....

....

....

....

10.   I made up a lie.

....
....
....
....

You can find the answers at the end of this section.

Answers:

Task 1

1.   *Transitive*

2.   *Transitive*

3.   *Intransitive*

4.   *Transitive*

5.   *Intransitive*

6.   *Intransitive*

7.   *Intransitive*

8.   *Transitive*

Task 2

1.   *He is so creative; he made up a story for his daughter and her friends.*

2.   *I have to fill out this form so I can go to university.*

3.   *Can you help me hang up this picture?*

4.   *There was a problem with his essay; he had left out a conclusion.*

5.   *The old friends ran into each other on the street.*

6.   I don't like how she looks down on everyone.

7.   We tried on the costumes but we looked awful in them!

8.   She takes after her grandmother.

9.   My mother says I have to get rid of my old toys.

10.   I can't hear anything - please turn up the volume!

Task 3

1.   She put out the fire.

She put the fire out.

She put it out.

2.   I called off the party.

I called the party off.

I called it off.

3.   Oscar asked out Samantha.

Oscar asked Samantha out.

Oscar asked her out.

4.   *They handed in their essays on time.*

They handed their essays in on time.

They handed them in on time.

5.   *I like showing off my new boots.*

I like showing my new boots off.

I like showing them off.

6.   *Turn off the washing machine!*

Turn the washing machine off!

Turn it off!

7.   *I have to drop off my sister at a party.*

I have to drop my sister off at a party.

I have to drop her off at a party.

8.   *She won't give up her love of singing.*

She won't give her love of singing up.

She won't give it up.

9.   *Put on your hat.*

Put your hat on.

Put it on.

10.   *I made up a lie.*

I made a lie up.

I made it up.

CHAPTER 11. TYPES OF PHRASAL VERBS (PART 2)

Phrasal verbs can be frustrating to learn. They often bear little resemblance to the main verb and there are so many to learn with different meanings.

The best way to learn these is to learn 'clusters' of phrasal verbs.

For example, the verb 'take':

Phrasal Verb	Transitive/Intransitive? Separable/Inseparable?	Example	Meaning
take after	transitive, inseparable	With my brown eyes and black hair, I take after my mother.	Resemble
take back	intransitive, separable	You need to take this dress back to the shop.	Return
take care of	transitive, inseparable	1. She can't go on holiday; she has to take care of her little sister. 2. He can't afford a holiday; he has to take care of these bills first.	1. Provide care for 2. Accept responsibility for
take off	1. transitive, separable 2. transitive, separable 3. intransitive, inseparable	1. Take your hat off. 2. Holly took the day off because she was ill. 3. The rocket took off.	1. Remove 2. Arrange an absence from work 3. To leave or to depart (quickly)
take up	1. transitive, separable 2. transitive, separable	1. I've decided to take up knitting. 2. James took up two seats.	1. Begin a hobby 2. Occupy space

If you look in a large dictionary, you will be able to see the various phrasal verbs under the main verb. It is a good idea to learn these in groups.

Task 1

Match the phrasal verbs (1-6) with their meanings (a-f).

Phrasal Verbs with **"Put"**

Meanings:

a. Tolerate

b. Return to its rightful place

c. Allow someone to stay for the night

d. Save something for later

e. Postpone, delay

f. Wear something

1. Put away - Transitive, separable. **Example:** *I put away a little money each month for my savings.*

Meaning:
....
....

2. Put off - Transitive, separable. **Example:** *I keep putting off my homework because there are more fun things to do!*

Meaning:

....

....

3. Put on - Transitive, separable. **Example:** *It's cold outside so I suggest you put on your jacket.*

Meaning:

....

....

4. Put up- Transitive, separable. **Example:** *My aunt and uncle are coming to London so I'm putting them up for the night.*

Meaning:

....

....

5. Put up with- Transitive, inseparable. **Example:** *I cannot put up with this nonsense any longer!*

Meaning:

....

....

6. Put back- Transitive, inseparable. **Example:** *I'm not buying you that toy so put it back.*

Meaning:

....

....

You can find the answers at the end of this section.

Task 2

MORE PHRASAL VERBS WITH "PUT":

a. I´m prepared to **put up with** it for the time being.

b. The World Wildlife Fund **put out** a press release.

c. Don´t **put off** until tomorrow what can be done today.

d. After my dog was **put down**, I cried for days.

e. He began to **put away** all the toys he had taken out to play with.

f. The Trade Union council **put forward** a plan for national recovery.

g. My self-confidence has been undermined because my mother is always **putting me down**.

h. I´ve got nowhere to sleep! Could anybody **put me up**?

Match the phrasal verbs with their meanings. Put <u>one or two words</u> in each gap:

1. If you put something _____, you postpone it until a later time.

2. If you put something _____, you replace it somewhere tidily.

3. If you put an animal _____, you kill it because it is too old or it is in too much pain.

4. If you put someone _____, you give them a bed for a night or two.

5. If you put _____ someone or something, you tolerate or accept them, even though that person or thing is disagreeable.

6. If you put someone _____, you criticize or humiliate them.

7. If you put _____an idea or a proposal, you state or publish it so people can consider and discuss it.

8. If a statement is put _____ to people, it is officially told to them.

Put a phrasal verb in each gap (!!!! Watch the tense)

1. I left my girlfriend because she´s always _____.

2. I _____ her moods if I were you.

3. If they _____ for the night, I would have had to sleep in the street.

4. Clinton has _____ a press release which contradicts his previous statements.

5. You needn't _____ the meeting: everybody could have made it in the end.

6. Every day, the government _____ a new plan to tackle unemployment.

7. If they find stray dogs in the streets, the poor animals _____.

8. As a child, I could never get used to _____ my things _____ after I had used them.

Task 3

In this conversation between two friends (Jim and Sasha), underline the phrasal verbs and write their meanings below. You may need to use a dictionary.

Jim: I meant to call in on my granddad today, but he passed away last night.

Sasha: Oh, I'm sorry Jim. Were you looking after him?

Jim: No, my grandma was. I think she liked taking care of him.

Sasha: Are you going to go over later, to see how she is?

Jim: Yes, I'll visit her later. She's with my parents at the moment. I'll have to find out what the plan is.

Sasha: Why don't you come over to my place? We can order pizza, or if you'd prefer, we can eat out.

Jim: Sure, that's a good idea. I'm looking forward to it.

1...
....

2...
....

3...
....

4...
....

5...
....

6..
....

7..
....

8..
....

9..
....

You can find the answers at the end of this section.

Three-Word Phrasal Verbs

We have already discussed four types of phrasal verbs:
transitive, intransitive, separable and inseparable. Most
of the phrasal verbs which we have studied in these sections
have been two part: they are made up of a main verb and a
preposition or an adverb. However, there are phrasal verbs
with two particles. These are called **three-word phrasal
verbs.**

Three-word Phrasal Verbs

These are **always transitive** due to the fact that they require
a direct object and they are **only inseparable.**

We have already seen a few three-word phrasal verbs, but
below are some additional ones for you to learn:

Phrasal Verb	Example	Meaning
Come up with	She came up with a great idea.	Contribute or think an idea, suggestion or plan
Get along with	He gets along with his dad.	Have a good relationship with
Talk back to	You must not talk back to your parents.	Answer impolitely to someone
Get away from	I need to book a holiday and get away with it all.	Take a break
Walk out on	I walked out on my family last year.	Abandon

Task 4:

The paragraph below does not use phrasal verbs. Using the three-word phrasal verbs from the table above, rewrite the story.

Three-word phrasal verbs from the table: *Come up with,*

get along with, talk back to, get away from, walk out on

I have never had a good relationship with my sister. She always answers impolitely to our parents. Last summer I grew sick of it. I needed to take a break from her, or I would go crazy! I thought of a plan that would help. I decided to abandon my family once and for all...

You can find the answers at the end of this section.

....

....

Task 5

Phrasal Verb	Meaning
Think back on	Recall
Look up to	Respect or admire
Cut down on	Curtail
Look out for	Be careful of
Make sure of	Verify

Using the three-word phrasal verbs in the table above (listed with their definitions), write the missing phrasal verbs in the sentences below.

Three-word phrasal verbs:

Think back on

Look up to

Cut down on

Look out for

Make sure of

1.   I am putting on weight, I need to
_____ my chocolate eating!

2.   She _____ her older brother.

3.   - Do you want to go on a walk in the countryside today?

   - Sure, but we'll have to _____ rattlesnakes!

4.   _____ the situation before you act.

5.   When I _____ our marriage, I remember all the good parts.

You can find the answers at the end of this section.

Answers:

Task 1

1. d

2. e

3. f

4. c

5. a

6. b

Task 2

1. If you put something off, you postpone it until a later time.

2. If you put something away, you place it somewhere tidily.

3. If you put an animal down, you kill it because it is too old or it is in too much pain.

4. If you put someone up, you give them a bed for a night or two.

5. If you put up with someone or something, you tolerate or accept them, even though that person or thing is annoying or unpleasant.

6. If you put someone down, you criticize or humiliate them.

7. If you put forward an idea or a proposal, you state or publish it so people can consider and discuss it.

8. If a statement is put out to people, it is officially told to them.

Put a phrasal verb in each gap (Watch the tense)

1. I left my girlfriend because she's always putting me down.

2. I wouldn't put up with her moods if I were you.

3. If they hadn't put me up for the night, I would have had to sleep in the street.

4. Clinton has put out a press release which contradicts his previous statements.

5. You needn't have put off the meeting: everybody could have made it in the end.

6. Every day, the government puts forward a new plan to tackle unemployment.

7. If they find stray dogs in the streets, the poor animals are put down.

8. As a child, I could never get used to putting my things away after I had used them.

Task 3

1. *call in on - visit*

2. *passed away - died*

3. *looking after - care for*

4. *taking care of - care for*

5. *go over - visit*

6. *find out - discover*

7. *come over - visit (the person being visited uses this)*

8. *eat out - eat at a restaurant instead of home*

9. *looking forward to - anticipate with pleasure*

Task 4

I have never gotten along with my sister. She always talks back to our parents. Last summer I grew sick of it. I needed to take a break from her, or I would go crazy! I thought of a plan that would help. I decided to abandon my family once and for all...

Task 5

1.   *I am putting on weight, I need to cut down on my chocolate eating!*

140

2.　　　*She looks up to her older brother.*

3.　　　*- Do you want to go on a walk in the countryside today?*

- Sure, but we'll have to look out for rattlesnakes!

4.　　　*Make sure of the situation before you act.*

5.　　　*When I think back on our marriage, I remember all the good parts.*

Chapter 12. Socialising

Phrasal verbs: socialising

ask (sb) out /ˌɑːsk ˈaʊt/
bump into /ˌbʌmp ˈɪntə/
catch up /ˌkætʃ ˈʌp/ (*past tense* & *past participle* caught)
chat (sb) up /ˌtʃæt ˈʌp/
dress up /ˌdres ˈʌp/
fall out /ˌfɔːl ˈaʊt/ (*past tense* fell, *past participle* fallen)
fit in /ˌfɪt ˈɪn/ (*past tense* & *past participle* fit)
get together /ˌget təˈgeðə/ (*past tense* & *past participle* got)
hang out /ˌhæŋ ˈaʊt/ (*past tense* & *past participle* hung)
hit it off /ˌhɪt ˌɪt ˈɒf/ (*past tense* & *past participle* hit)
meet up /ˌmiːt ˈʌp/ (*past tense* & *past participle* met)
turn up /ˌtɜːn ˈʌp/

Exercise 1

Match the phrasal verbs with the definitions. You may need to use a dictionary.

1. fall out

2. bump into

3. hit it off

4. ask someone out

5. turn up

6. hang out

like someone when you first meet

quarrel or fight (with someone)

arrive to or attend an event

meet (someone) by chance

invite someone to a place with romantic intentions.

spend a lot of time with someone

EXERCISE 2

CHOOSE THE CORRECT PHRASAL VERBS TO COMPLETE THE PARAGRAPH. WRITE THE WORDS IN THE BLANKS.

The other day I (1) asked out / bumped into an old friend of mine, Joe Burton, while I was at the supermarket. I hadn't seen him for ages. I wanted to (2) catch up / hit it off with him, so I suggested going for a beer.

Unfortunately, Joe was very busy, so he didn't have time for a beer. *'Let's (3) chat you up / meet up later in the week'*, I said. Joe looked in his phone and said, *'why don't we (4) fit in / get together for lunch at 12.30 on Wednesday at the Red Lion pub?'*.

It's not a very formal place, so I didn't need to (5) dress up / hang out for the occasion. I got to the pub about 15 minutes late, so I was slightly stressed. By the time Joe (6) fell out / turned up I'd finished my second beer and I was starving. He was almost an hour late!

EXERCISE 3

Use the other phrasal verbs from the previous activity to complete the paragraph.

Ask out/ hit it off/chat up/fit in/hand out/fall out

I remember how I met my girlfriend. I used to (1) .... with a group of mates every weekend. One day, my best friend Georgie came along with his sister Mary and her friend Anna. Both Mary and Anna were about the same age as we were. Anna had nothing in common with my friends, so she didn't (2)............. However, Mary, loved football and music, and I (3)............... with her immediately.

I (4)............... and she said yes, so I was thrilled. We went to a nice pub near the lake without the others. A guy at the bar tried to (5)............... when I went to the toilet but she turned him down, which made me smile!

Soon after that, I (6)............... with Georgie and we didn't speak again for a few months because he owed me money and never paid me back. We have now forgotten about it though and we are friends again.

Answers

EXERCISE 1

1. fall out- quarrel or fight (with someone)

2. bump into- meet (someone) by chance

3. hit it off- like someone when you first meet

4. ask someone out- invite someone to a place with romantic intentions.

5. turn up- arrive to or attend an event

6. hang out- spend a lot of time with someone

EXERCISE 2

The other day I (1) bumped into an old friend of mine, Joe Burton, while I was at the supermarket. I hadn't seen him for ages. I wanted to (2) catch up with him, so I suggested going for a beer.

Unfortunately, Joe was very busy, so he didn't have time for a beer. 'Let's (3) meet up later in the week', I said. Joe looked in his phone and said, ' why don't we (4) get together for lunch at 12.30 on Wednesday at the Red Lion pub?'.

It's not a very formal place, so I didn't need to (5) dress up for the occasion. I got to the pub about 15 minutes late, so I was

*slightly stressed. By the time Joe (6) turned up I'd finished my
second beer and I was starving. He was almost an hour late!*

Exercise 3

Ask out/ hit it off/chat up/fit in/hand out/fall out

*I remember how I met my girlfriend. I used to (1) hang out
with a group of mates every weekend. One day, my best friend
Georgie came along with his sister Mary and her friend Anna.
Both Mary and Anna were about the same age as we were.
Anna had nothing in common with my friends, so she didn't (2)
fit in. However, Mary, loved football and music, and I (3)hit it
off with her immediately.*

*I (4) asked her out and she said yes, so I was thrilled. We went
to a nice pub near the lake without the others. A guy at the bar
tried to (5) chat her up when I went to the toilet but she
turned him down, which made me smile!*

*Soon after that, I (6) fell out with Georgie and we didn't speak
again for a few months, because he owed me money and never
paid me back. We have now forgotten about it though and we
are friends again.*

Phrasal Verb Exercises

Phrasal Verbs Exercise 1

Do the phrasal verb quizzes here to see how many you know. You may need to look back at previous chapters or consult a dictionary.

Come back to the quiz a week or two later and see if you still remember them!

Choose the answer A, B, C or D that completes each sentence. There are FIVE questions in all.

1) If you don't study, you will .... up in a poorly paid job

come

end

save

rise

147

2) If an arrangement, plan, or deal .... through, it fails to happen

Falls

comes

goes

lets

3) She's smart enough to .... out what to do

raise

think

figure

see
148

4) If you .... out a form or other document requesting information, you write information in the spaces on it

write

note

complete

fill

5) If you ....something out, you learn something that you did not already know, especially by making a deliberate effort to do so.

pull

push

149

see

find

Phrasal Verbs Exercise 2

Choose the answer A, B, C or D that completes each sentence. There are FIVE questions in all.

1) The film was OK but it didn't really .... up to all the hype.

    come

    live

    grow

    look

2) It's tearing me .... to see my two best friends arguing so much. I wish they'd sort their differences out and start being friendly with each other again.

    apart

    up

    out

through

3) This is a real bargain. You should snap it .... while you have the chance.

out

in

back

up

4) We really do need to get another car. This one keeps .... down.

breaking

taking

falling

cutting

5) You never wanted to take that job. Don't .... out you're disappointed you failed the interview.

work

set

put

make

Vocabulary Notes:

If you make out that something is the case or make something out to be the case, you try to cause people to believe that it is true when in reality it isn't. .

If you snap something up, you buy it quickly because it is cheap or is just what you want

If someone or something lives up to what they were expected to be, they are as good as they were expected to be.

If a machine or a vehicle breaks down, it stops working.

If something tears you apart, it makes you feel very upset, worried, and unhappy.

Sex, Dating & Relationships

Read the text and underline the phrasal verbs you find. Try to guess the meaning from the text and then check the definitions in the phrasal verb notes below.

If you are single and you like someone who is also single, you might think about chatting him or her up, or flirting with them, which is very similar. When you chat someone up, it shows that you are keen on that person. It's often a good idea to ask the person out if you think that he or she is also keen on you. If you are going out with someone and you go off him or her, then after a while it might be a good idea break up or split up.

Splitting up with your partner is often a good idea if you think that you will both be happier outside of the relationship.

However, if you normally get on like a house on fire and you have a lot in common, it might be a better idea to work through your problems so that you can be happy together and that way you don't need to split up.

Phrasal Verb Notes:

To chat someone up is to flirt with them as you speak. The objective is to get to know the person better in a romantic way.

When you are keen on someone you like them and you are attracted to him or her.

Ask someone out is to invite someone for dinner, to the cinema or to an event when you are attracted to that person and you want to get to know him or her better.

To be going out with someone is a stage of romantic relationships where two people meet socially, each with the objective of evaluating the other person's suitability as a prospective partner in an intimate relationship or marriage

To go off someone is when you stop liking that person.

To split up or break up with someone is when you stop a relationship with a person.

To get on, get along or get on well with someone is to have a good relationship with that person. It can be romantically or as friends.

To get on like a house on fire is to have an excellent relationship with someone. It can be romantically or as friends.

To have a lot in common with someone is when your personalities, experiences or objectives in life are similar. This builds a good basis for a good relationship.

To work through a problem is to try to solve it.

Exercise 3

Now insert the phrasal verbs and expressions into the gaps in the text below. You can use the same expression more than once and you may not need to use all expressions:

A)   to chat a girl / boy up

B)   to be keen on (sbdy)

C)   to be engaged to (sbdy)

D)   to go off (sbdy)

E)   to leave (sbdy)

F)   to ask a girl / boy out

G)   to be good friends

H)   to get married to (sbdy)

I)   to be going out with (sbdy)

J)   to get on well with (sbdy) (to get on like a house on fire with someone)

K)   to be fond of (sbdy)

L)   to be in love with (sbdy)

M)   to split up with (sbdy)

N)   to separate from (sbdy)

O)   to get divorced from (sbdy)

P)   to have a lot in common with (sbdy)

Q)   to take someone out

Stages of love – phrasal verbs gap fill

Stages of Love.

Bill fancied Susan the first moment he caught sight of her across a crowded discotheque. Although he was quite shy, he decided to go over and_____1 her_____. She was very friendly and easy to talk to, so he asked her if she wanted to_____2 him. She agreed, and a few nights later, he_____3 to dinner at a very expensive restaurant. They had a wonderful evening together and realised that they_____4 each other.

After that they started seeing each other on a regular basis and before long, Bill knew that he_____5 Susan. She felt the same way about him so they decided to_____6.

Four weeks before the wedding Susan met a handsome sailor called Tom and started_____7 him. She wanted to_____8 her engagement to Bill, but she didn't know how to tell him.

Eventually, a week before the wedding, Susan told Bill the truth. He was heartbroken! They_____9 the wedding and they haven't seen each other since.

157

Susan and Tom didn't stay together for very long. They kept on having arguments and finally they_____10. As for poor Bill, he still thinks about Susan and the life they could have had together.

Answers

Chapter 6- Phrasal Verbs Exercise 1

1. If you don't study, you will end up in a poorly paid job

2. If an arrangement, plan, or deal falls through, it fails to happen

3. She's smart enough to figure out what to do

4. If you fill out a form or other document requesting information, you write information in the spaces on it

5. If you find something out, you learn something that you did not already know, especially by making a deliberate effort to do so.

Chapter 6- Phrasal Verbs Exercise 2

1. Live

2. Apart

3. Up

4. Breaking

5. Make

Chapter 6- Phrasal Verbs Exercise 3

Stages of Love.

Bill fancied Susan the first moment he caught sight of her across a crowded club. Although he was quite shy, he decided to go over and CHAT 1 her UP. She was very friendly and easy to talk to, so he asked her if she wanted to GO OUT WITH 2 him. She agreed, and a few nights later, he TOOK HER OUT 3 to dinner at a very expensive restaurant. They had a wonderful evening together and realised that they HAD A LOT IN COMMON WITH 4 each other.

After that they started seeing each other on a regular basis and before long, Bill knew that he WAS IN LOVE WITH 5 Susan. She felt the same way about him so they decided to GET MARRIED 6.

Four weeks before the wedding Susan met a handsome sailor called Tom and started GO OUT WITH 7 him. She wanted to BREAK OFF 8 her engagement to Bill, but she didn't know how to tell him.

Eventually, a week before the wedding, Susan told Bill the truth. He was heartbroken! They BROKE OFF 9 the wedding and they haven't seen each other since.

Susan and Tom didn't stay together for very long. They kept on having arguments and finally they SPLIT UP 10. As for poor Bill, he still thinks about Susan and the life they could have had together.

Chapter 13. Phrasal Verbs with 'Take'

Mini-Dictionary

Phrasal Verbs with 'take'

Here is a list with some examples of the most common phrasal verbs with 'take'. Use this glossary to complete exercises at the end of this chapter.

Take aback- Meaning: Surprise or shock -Example: *It took me aback when she asked such a personal question.*

Take after- Meaning: To have similar appearance, character or personality to an older family member- Example*: She takes after her father.*

Take against- Meaning: Stop liking someone; to become hostile toward- Example: *She took against Mary when she was promoted over her.*

Take apart- Meaning: Separate something into its parts- Example: *The mechanic took the car apart to find the problem.*

Take aside- Meaning: Get someone alone to talk to them- Example: *John was taken aside by the manager when he shouted at a customer. .*

Take away- Meaning: Remove something and put it in a different place- Example: *My dad took our plates away and came back with chocolate cake for dessert!*

Take away- Meaning: Remove something, either material or abstract, so that a person no longer has it- Example: *Jack's mum took his computer away until he improved at school.*

Take away- Meaning: Subtract or diminish something- Example: *If I have three oranges and I take away two, how many oranges do I have left? The answer is …. one.*

Take away- Meaning: Leave a memory or impression in one's mind that you think about later- Example*: I took away the impression that the manager did not get along with his players.*

Take away- Meaning: Force someone to leave a place and take him or her somewhere else -Example: *The police took the suspect to the station for questioning.*

Take away from- Meaning: Make something seem worse, not so good or less interesting- Example: *His behavior took away from the excitement of the party.*

Take back- Meaning: Retract something you said earlier. - Example: *You are not selfish; I take it back, I'm sorry.*

Take back- Meaning: When something makes you remember some past event or time we say that it 'takes you back'- Example: *That film takes me back to when I was a kid at Christmas.*

Take back- Meaning: Start a relationship again with someone after you have split up- Example: *Jane has forgiven Aaron, and taken him back despite his behavior.*

Take back- Meaning: Regain possession of something - Example: *I'm taking back my laptop because you are always using it without asking!*

Take back- Meaning: Return something to a shop for a refund or exchange- Example: *These shoes are too small, I'm going to have to take them back to the shop tomorrow.*

Take down- Meaning: Remove something from a wall or similar vertical surface to which it is fixed or handing position- Example: *She took down the photograph and replaced it with the framed picture.*

Take down- Meaning: Make notes, especially to record something spoken- Example: *If you have a pen, you should take down the most important points of the lecture.*

Take down- Meaning: Remove a temporary structure - Example: When everything else is ready, we can take down the gazebo.

Take down- Meaning: Lower an item of clothing without removing it- Example: *The nurse asked me to take down my trousers.*

Take for- Meaning. Think of or regard as- Example: *What do you take me for, a fool?*

Take for- Meaning: to get confused about what something or who someone is- Example: *Sorry, I took you for someone else, you look like a friend of mine.-*

Take for (also 'take in for', 'take for a ride', 'rip off' or 'do' someone)- Meaning: Defraud; Example: *Jane is very upset because the scammers took her for 500 pounds.*

Take in- Meaning: Shorten (a piece of clothing) or make it smaller- Example*: I asked the tailor to take the trousers in a bit around the leg.*

Take in- Meaning: Absorb information or understand the reality of that information- Example: *He was in shock after the incident, so it took him a while to take the news in.*

Take in- Meaning: Deceive, give a false impression- Example: *Everyone was taken in by his lies.*

Take it out on- Meaning: Unleash one's anger on [a person or thing other than the one that caused it]- Example: *Don't take it out on me just because you're in a bad mood.*

Take it upon oneself- Meaning: Assume personal responsibility for a task or action- Example: *She took it upon herself to ring him and ask him to come over.*

Take off- Meaning: To remove something, usually clothes or accessories- Example: *The doctor asked me to take off my shirt.*

Take off- Meaning: Imitate, often in a comical manner - Example: *John Kraven is a comedian who takes off all the famous people in my country.*

Take off- Meaning: When an aircraft leaves the ground and begins to fly; to ascend into the air- Example: *The helicopter took off at 6pm.*

165

Take off- Meaning: to become successful or grow- Example: The project has really taken off this year, we are very excited.

Take off- Meaning: to leave- Example: *We have to take off now or we are going to be late.*

Take on- Meaning: introduce, bring in or acquire - Example: *The truck took on 50 pallets in Southampton this morning.*

Take on- Meaning: employ, bring in - Example: *When the number of customers increased, we had to take on more staff.*

Take on- Meaning: Begin to have or exhibit physical traits- Example: *He took on the appearance of a criminal for the role in his new movie.*

Take on- Meaning: Take responsibility or burden- Example: *I'll take on the extra work if you can manage the project.*

Take on- Meaning: Attempt to fight or compete with- Example: *They took on the most notorious gang members in the city and they won.*

Take out-Meaning: Remove- Example: *Please take out the rubbish before the kitchen starts to smell!*

Take out- Meaning: Invite someone out socially, often for romantic reasons- Example: *Let me take you out for a drink*

Take over- Meaning: Adopt a responsibility or duty from someone else- Example: He will take over the job permanently when the accountant retires.

Take over- Meaning: Take control of something for someone temporarily- Example: *Can you take over driving for half an hour while I get some shut-eye (sleep)?*

Take over- Meaning: Buy the control of a business- Example: *Rola Cola PLC is planning to take over Punjabi MC Ltd this month.*

Take over- Meaning: Take control by conquest or invasion- Example: *Germany took over half of Europe leading up to WW2. (Note: "Lead up to" means "in the events which caused and which came before")*

Take to- Meaning: Adapt to; to learn, grasp or master something- Example: *He took to gold instantly, he was a natural. (Note: "a natural" means someone who has natural talent at something)*

Take to- Meaning: to go into or move towards- Example: *As we drove through field, dozens of birds took to the air, scared by the noise of the car.*

Take up- Meaning: to start doing (an activity) regularly - Example: *I'm thinking of taking up tennis once a week.*

Take up- Meaning: to start to talk about an issue or problem with someone- Example: *I took my concerns up with the manager.*

Take up- Meaning: Occupy; to consume (space or time)- Example: *The sofa takes up half the living room.*

Take up- Meaning: Accept a proposal or offer- Example:

John: *Next time you're in town, I'll buy you a beer.*

167

James: *I'll take you up on that!*

Take through- Meaning: Explain in steps; give a tour of a place- Example: *Let me take you through the basics of how to cook Southern Fried Chicken*

Exercise 1

For each of the six questions choose the one correct answer. You might need to check the glossary above.

1. When his partner retires, he's planning to take ____ the business in Sydney.

a. off

b. after

c. up

d. over

2. Our helicopter took ___ 4 hours late!

a. over

b. up

c. off

d. after

168

3. Why do so many people take ___ a sport in the winter?

a. over

b. off

c. up

d. after

4. Janice is often irritable, she takes ___ her mum.

a. over

b. off

c. in

d. after

5. When she found out he had left, initially she couldn't take it ___.

a. after

b. over

c. in

d. off

6. I was completely taken ___ when he told me he was working late at the office.

a. after

b. in

c. over

d. after

Exercise 2

1 Match each sentence beginning 1 - 10 with an appropriate ending a) – j).

1 She is very similar to her mother, whereas her sister takes

2 The new CEO is very serious and we haven't really taken

3 I need to remember this lesson. I'll get a pen and paper and take

4 My feet are swollen. I think I'll take

5 This jumper is too big. I need to take

6 When my mum retired, I took

7 Michael's become inseparable from his bike since he took

8 You should get rid of this table. It's a small room and it takes

9 We have too much to do at work. We need to take

170

10 I thought I could manage this job, but I think I've taken

a) it back.

b) on more staff

c) on too much

d) up half the room.

e) up cycling.

f) off my shoes.

g) over the family business.

h) to her.

i) after her father.

j) down the most important parts.

Exercise 3

Now write the infinitive of each of the phrasal verbs with 'take' from exercise 2 next to its meaning below.

a) accept the responsibility for something _____

b) start a new hobby or activity _____

c) start to like or feel good about _____

d) to employ (give a job to) _____

171

e) remind or provoke memories _____

f) to become successful _____

g) make notes _____

h) to be similar in appearance or personality _____

i) take control of   _____

j) occupy space or time   _____

Answers:

Exercise 1

1:

A. 'TAKE OFF' USUALLY REFERS TO PLANES OR CLOTHES!

B. 'TAKE AFTER' MEANS 'SIMILAR TO'.

C. 'TAKE UP' MEANS BEGIN A SPORT OR HOBBY.

D. CORRECT

2:

A. 'TAKE OVER' USUALLY MEANS TAKE CONTROL OF.

B. 'TAKE UP' MEANS BEGIN A SPORT OR HOBBY.

C. CORRECT

D. 'TAKE AFTER' MEANS 'SIMILAR TO'.

3:

A. 'TAKE OVER' USUALLY MEANS TAKE CONTROL OF.

B. 'TAKE OFF' USUALLY REFERS TO PLANES OR CLOTHES!

C. CORRECT

D. 'TAKE AFTER' MEANS 'SIMILAR TO'.

4:

A. 'Take over' usually means take control of.

B. 'Take off' usually refers to planes or clothes!

C. 'Take in' means to try to understand something or to fool someone.

D. Correct

5:

A. 'Take after' means 'similar to'.

B. 'Take over' usually means take control of.

C. Correct

D. 'Take off' usually refers to planes or clothes!

6:

A. 'Take after' means 'similar to'.

B. Correct

C. 'Take over' usually means take control of.

D. 'Take after' means 'similar to'.

Exercise 2

1 She is very similar to her mother, whereas her sister takes after her father.

2 The new CEO is very serious and we haven't really taken to her.

3 I need to remember this lesson. I'll get a pen and paper and take down the most important parts.

4 My feet are swollen. I think I'll take off my shoes.

5 This jumper is too big. I need to take it back.

6 When my mum retired, I took over the family business.

7 Michael's become inseparable from his bike since he took up cycling.

8 You should get rid of this table. It's a small room and it takes up half the room.

9 We have too much to do at work. We need to take on more staff.

10 I thought I could manage this job, but I think I've taken on too much.

Exercise 3

a) accept the responsibility for something – Take on

b) start a new hobby or activity – Take up

c) start to like or feel good about – Take to

d) to employ (give a job to) – Take on

e) remind or provoke memories – Take back

f) to become successful – Take off

g) make notes   - Take down

h) to be similar in appearance or personality- Take after

i) take control of- Take over

j) occupy space or time- Take up

Chapter 14. Phrasal Verbs with 'Put'

Mini-Dictionary

Phrasal Verbs with 'put'

Here is a list with some examples of the most common phrasal verbs with 'put'. Use this glossary to complete exercises at the end of this chapter.

Put out- Meaning: Extinguish a light or something which has fire. Example: *Put out your cigarette please, this is a no-smoking area.*

Put out- Meaning: Release or publish. Example: *We need to put out an email explaining the situation.*

Put (effort) into- Meaning: To try- Example: I put a lot of work into the presentation.

Put across- Meaning: Explain or communicate something clearly and understandably- Example: The way she put the message across was quite rude.

Put aside- Meaning: Save (money)- Example: *I try to put a few quid aside every day for our summer holiday. (Note: "quid" is slang for British pounds)*

Put aside- Meaning: Ignore or intentionally disregard (something), temporarily or permanently- Example: *We need to put our differences aside.*

Put away- Meaning: put something somewhere organised or out of sight. Example: *When I tidy my room I put all my clothes away.*

Put away- Meaning: Consume in large quantities (food and drink)- Example: *He put away 12 chicken wings, 2 steaks and a whole roast chicken.. What a beast!*

Put away- Meaning: Send to jail- Example: *They put her away for 2 years on weapons charges.*

Put back- Meaning: Return something to its original place- Example: She put the toys back in the cupboard.

Put back- Meaning: Postpone a meeting, event or appointment- Example: *The meeting has been put back to 2pm due to the storms.*

Put down- Meaning: Belittle, humiliate or demean- Example: *She´s not very nice, she constantly puts her husband down.*

Put down- Meaning: Pay a deposit or initial installment- Example: *She put down a 2,000 euro deposit.*

Put down- Meaning: Eliminate or stop by force- Example: *Government security forces quickly put down the civil unrest.*

Put down- Meaning: Kill an animal because it is sick or suffering.- Example: *We had to put our dog down last month because he was too ill.*

Put down- Meaning: Write (something)- Example: *Put down your name and address on this paper.*

Put down- Meaning: Finish a phone-call; to hang up-
Example: *Don't put the phone down please, I want to apologise to you!*

Put down- Meaning: Add a name to a list- Example: *I've put myself down on the VIP list for the party. .*

Put down or Putting up- Meaning: Make prices, or taxes, lower or higher- Example: *The Chinese government are putting up the price of oil in order to stimulate the use of renewable energies.*

Put down- Meaning: Place a baby somewhere to sleep-
Example: *I have just put Charley down so please be quiet!*

Put down (a book)- Meaning: Stop, temporarily or permanently, reading (a book)- Example: *I can't put this book down, it's so interesting!*

Put down as- Meaning: Make assumptions about someone's personality. - Example*: I put her down as an arrogant, materialistic snob, but she is actually very sweet.*

Put down for- Meaning: Put someone on a list of people who have offered to help, or contribute to something- Example: *Put Jack down to help with the cleaning, he told me he wanted to do it.*

Put down to- Meaning: assume or come to the conclusion about the cause of a situation- Example: *We often put high crime rates down to high unemployment.*

Put on- Meaning: To fake or pretend. Example: *He puts on funny accents to make us laugh.*

Put on (clothes)- Meaning: To fit clothes on your body. Example: *It´s really sunny, I need to put my hat on!*

Put on- Meaning: To blame someone else for something. Example: *You can´t put that on me, it wasn´t my fault!*

Put on (weight)- Meaning: To gain weight or fat. Example: *I have put on at least 2 stone over Christmas. I didn´t stop eating!*

Put forward (a suggestion or idea)- Meaning: Propose for consideration- Example: *The CEO put forward new plans to reduce costs.*

Put forward- Meaning: Change the time in a time zone to a later time. Example: *I almost forgot that we have to put the clocks forward tomorrow by 1 hour.*

Put up with- Meaning: Tolerate. Example: *I'm too tired to put up with him, his attitude annoys me.*

Put up- Meaning: Offer accommodation for the night. Example: *My parents put us up while our house was being re-furbished.*

Put up- Meaning: raise. Example: *Put your hands up in the air like you just don´t care!*

Put someone up to something- Meaning: manipulate someone or convince them to do something. Example: *Did Mary put you up to this? I told her I didn´t want to talk about my problem.*

Put off- Meaning: Distract. Example: *Don´t try to put me off the game, that´s cheating!*

Put off- Meaning: Delay. Example: *We put off the show because of the rain.*

Put someone off something or someone- Meaning: Make someone stop liking something or someone. Example: *Her lack of a sense of humour put me off her, so I didn't ask her out*

. .

Exercise 1

Phrasal verbs with 'put'

Match each sentence beginning 1 - 12 with an appropriate ending a) – l).

1. It's raining quite heavily. You should put on
2. I didn't recognize her when I saw her because she had put on
3. There's nothing good on TV. Why don't we put on
4. She might need to move. Her landlady has put up
5. We need to put up new
6. Put your hand up
7. My parents offered to put
8. How do you put up
9. We had to put off the meeting
10. It snowed so heavily that it put us off
11. I could never concentrate at university, because all
12. We need to put out

a) us up for the weekend when we go to visit.

b) a lot of weight.

181

c) because the CEO was stuck in traffic.

d) with her constant moaning?

e) your new coat.

f) the fire before it spreads.

g) going out, so we watched a film instead.

h) the parties and the noise put me off.

i) her rent.

j) an online film?

k) curtains because the old ones have holes in them.

l) if you have any questions.

Exercise 2

Now decide which phrasal verb is needed in each sentence:

1. I can't ___ her anymore, she's driving me bonkers! *(Note: to drive someone bonkers means to drive him or her crazy- to annoy)*

Put on

Put back

Put up with

2. Please __ the bread when you're finished using it.

Put back

Put on

Put down

3. Can you __ the conference until Friday please?

Put up

Put off

Put down

4. She __ all the time, but he's still married to her.

Puts him up

Puts him across

Puts him down

5. They __ a new blog post every week. It's really good.

Put up with

Put down

Put out

6. I was trying to ___ my opinion but no one listened.

Put away

Put across

Put up with

Answers:

Exercise 1

1. It's raining quite heavily. You should put on your new coat.
2. I didn't recognize her when I saw her because she had put on a lot of weight.
3. There's nothing good on TV. Why don't we put on an online film?
4. She might need to move. Her landlady has put up her rent.
5. We need to put up new curtains because the old ones have holes in them.
6. Put your hand up if you have any questions.
7. My parents offered to put us up for the weekend when we go to visit.
8. How do you put up with her constant moaning?
9. We had to put off the meeting because the CEO was stuck in traffic.
10. It snowed so heavily that it put us off going out, so we watched a film instead.
11. I could never concentrate at university, because all the parties and the noise put me off.
12. We need to put out the fire before it spreads.

Exercise 2

1. I can't __ her anymore, she's driving me bonkers! *(Note: to drive someone bonkers means to drive him or her crazy- to annoy)*

Put on

Put back

Put up with

2. Please ___ the bread when you're finished using it.

Put back

Put on

Put down

3. Can you ___ the conference until Friday please?

Put up

Put off

Put down

4. She ___ all the time, but he's still married to her.

Puts him up

Puts him across

Puts him down

5. They ___ a new blog post every week. It's really good.

Put up with

Put down

Put out

6. I was trying to ___ my opinion but no one listened.

Put away

Put across

Put up with

Chapter 15. Phrasal Verbs with 'Get'

Mini-Dictionary

Phrasal Verbs with 'get'

Here is a list with some examples of the most common phrasal verbs with 'get'. Use this glossary to complete exercises at the end of this chapter.

get across (separable) – to communicate clearly- Example: *The man was so stubborn that we couldn´t get the message across and change his mind.*

get ahead (intransitive - no object) – to make progress- Example: *She needs to work hard in life if she wishes to be successful.*

get along (get on) (intransitive) – to have a good relationship- Example: *I get along very well with my grandfather. We have similar personalities.*

get around (1)- (inseparable) – to avoid or to overcome a problem, a rule, or a challenge- Example: *Walter got around the rules by pretending he didn´t know about them.*

get around (2)- (intransitive - no object) – to go from place to place- Example: Since he lives in the city centre, he gets around everywhere on foot.

get around to (3) – to finally do something- Example: *We finally got round to clearing the loft after three months!*

get at- (intransitive - no object) – to hint or to mean- Example: *What are you getting at? Can you be more specific and give me an example?*

get at– to reach so that you can take something- Example: *Can you pass me that bottle please? I can´t get at it because I´m too short.*

get away- (intransitive - no object) – to escape- Example: *The prisoners got away through a hole in the wall.*

get away with something– to escape responsibility- Example: *We got away with not doing our homework because we told the teacher that our dog had eaten it.*

get back- (intransitive - no object) – to return- Example: *Jeremy always gets back late from the office. He has a very intense job.*

get by- (intransitive - no object) – to survive- Example: *When we were young my family had no money, but we got by.*

get down (to)- (intransitive - no object) – to concentrate or focus on a task. - Example: *Let´s get down to business. We need to find a solution to the supply problem. .*

get down (1)- (separable) – to discourage- Example: *Don´t let the rain get you down!*

get down (2)- (separable) – to put in writing- Example: *Please Bob, can you get the minutes down during the meeting?*

get in- (intransitive - no object) – to arrive- Example: *The bus got in an hour early because of the mistake in the timetable.*

get off (1)- (inseparable) – to leave- Example: *I forgot my hat when I got off the train.*

get off (2)- (intransitive - no object) – to receive lesser punishment- Example: *He crashed his car into a shop window because he was on his phone, but he got off with just a small fine and some community service.*

get off (3)- (separable) – to interrupt- Example: *We have the day off today because of the floods. We don´t have to go to work!*

get out (1)- (intransitive - no object) – to spread- Example: *Word gets out quickly in our small village, so everyone knew Michael was planning on proposing to Jess.*

get out (of) (2)- (inseparable) – to escape- Example: *Joe always has an excuse and gets out of cleaning the car.*

get out (of) (3)- (inseparable) – to leave- Example: *Let's get out of here.. I´m hot and tired!*

get over- (inseparable) – to recover- Example: *It took Jill some time to get over her divorce.*

get rid of- (inseparable) – dispose of something or dismiss someone- Example: *Please get rid of that old bike. It's so dirty*

get through (1)- (inseparable) – to finish- Example: *We need to get through at least 6 pages of material in today´s lesson.*

get through (2)- (inseparable) – to communicate a message effectively- Example: *We need to get through to him before he does something stupid, but he doesn´t listen.*

get to (1)- (inseparable) – to annoy- Example: *His comments got to me!*

get to (2)- (inseparable) – to arrive - Example: *What time will you get to the station?*

get together- (intransitive - no object) – to meet up with someone - Example: *They got together for a drink and 6 months later they were married!*

get up- (intransitive - no object) – wake up and get out of bed - Example: *My new job starts at 8 am so I have to get up at 6 o´clock.*

get up to– to do - Example: *What did you get up to yesterday?*

Exercise 1

Read the sentences below. Underline the phrasal verbs and try to work out the meaning from the context. Then complete the gaps below each sentence using one of the following meanings.

to communicate a message effectively

to reach so that you can take something

to communicate clearly

to escape responsibility

to avoid or to overcome a problem, a rule, or a challenge

to escape

to discourage

to recover

1) They realised it would be a difficult challenge, but after a lot of hard work they got around it.

Phrasal Verb: ....

Meaning: ....

2) I can never get at the top shelf in the supermarket, so I always have to ask for help. I wish I were taller.

Phrasal Verb: ....

Meaning: ....

3) After Jim had made several unsuccessful attempts to get through to Sally, he realized she wasn't listening, so he went home.

Phrasal Verb: ....

Meaning: ....

4) Albert managed to get away from the meeting early for Mary's birthday.

Phrasal Verb: ....

Meaning: ....

5) My girlfriend left me last month and I felt very sad, but I've got over it now.

Phrasal Verb: ....

Meaning: ....

6) I don't like sad films, they really get me down.

Phrasal Verb: ....

Meaning: ....

7) Jason is a good presenter who always gets his message across.

Phrasal Verb: ....

Meaning: ....

8) The police didn´t catch the thief, so he got away with it.

Phrasal Verb: ....

Meaning: ....

Answers:

1) They realised it would be a difficult challenge, but after a lot of hard work they got around it.

get around

to avoid or to overcome a problem, a rule, or a challenge

2) I can never get at the top shelf in the supermarket, so I always have to ask for help. I wish I were taller.

get at

to reach so that you can take something

3) After Jim had made several unsuccessful attempts to get through to Sally, he realized she wasn't listening, so he went home.

get through–

to communicate a message effectively

4) Albert managed to get away from the meeting early for Mary's birthday.

get away-

to escape

5) My girlfriend left me last month and I felt very sad, but I've got over it now.

get over-

to recover

6) I don't like sad films, they really get me down.

get down

to discourage

7) Jason is a good presenter who always gets his message across.

get across–

to communicate clearly

8) The police didn't catch the thief, so he got away with it.

get away with–

to escape responsibility

Chapter 16. Phrasal Verbs with 'Come'

Mini-Dictionary

Phrasal Verbs with 'come'

Here is a list with some examples of the most common phrasal verbs with 'come'. Use this glossary to complete exercises at the end of this chapter.

come across (1)- (inseparable) – to find- Example: *I came across a very interesting book while browsing the second-hand bookshops in Manchester.*

come across (2)- (inseparable) – to give the impression or appearance- Example: *He came across quite arrogant at first but he was a nice guy.*

come along (1)- (intransitive - no object) – to progress- Example: *How is her assignment coming along?*

come along (2)- (intransitive - no object) – to casually attend or appear somewhere- Example: *When Jenny came along after work, Robbie left because he was still angry with her.*

come around- (intransitive - no object) – to change opinions- Example: *After hours of arguing he finally came round (he agreed with me)*

come back (1)- (inseparable) -- to return- Example: *Madison comes back from London tomorrow. We need to pick her up from the airport at 2.*

come back (2)- (inseparable) -- to remember- when a memory returns because of something you see, hear or feel- Example: *It all came back to me when I saw the ring. I'd forgotten everything, but now I remember.*

come by- (inseparable) – to get or obtain- Example: *I came by this watch when I was walking along the beach and found it.*

come down (with)- (inseparable) – to become ill- Example: *Maybe you should go to the doctor's. This is the third time you've come down with a cold this month.*

come from- (inseparable) -- to originate- Example: *Madison comes from a wealthy family. Jack comes from England.*

come in- (inseparable) -- to finish- Example: *Madison came in last in the race, but she enjoyed herself.*

come into- (inseparable) -- to acquire- Example: *Madison came into money when she was 21, after her parents suddenly died.*

come off (1)- (intransitive - no object) – to give the impression- Example: *Jack comes off as a hard person, but in fact he is quite caring.*

come off (2)- (intransitive - no object) – to stop taking a drug or medication- Example: *Mick is coming off drugs, he has a serious addiction.*

come on- (intransitive - no object) – to give the impression- Example: *Jack comes on as a hard person, but in fact he is quite caring.*

come on- (intransitive - no object) – to start to work (water, electricity etc..)- Example: *The electricity came back on two hours after the power cut.*

come out- (intransitive - no object) – to be revealed or to reveal information- Example: *The player's past came out when his old friends spoke to the press.*

come over- (intransitive - no object) – to visit causally or spontaneously- Example: *Come over for dinner tonight, we're having a Sunday roast!*

come through- (intransitive - no object) – to do what is expected- Example: *William came through only after Wanda begged him for three days to get the tickets for the game.*

come to- (inseparable) – to total (counting money)- Example: *The restaurant bill comes to 150 dollars*

come up- (intransitive - no object) – to be mentioned in conversation- Example: *The topic of his money problems came up during the conversation.*

come up with- (inseparable) – to invent or think about something new- Example: *Joe came up with a very good idea for the marketing campaign.*

come upon- (inseparable) – to discover by accident- Example: *While cleaning the house, we came upon an amazing picture from the 19th century.*

Exercise 1:

Write the correct preposition to make meaningful sentences.

1. Mary comes .... Ireland and she was born in Dublin.

2. Jason came .... last in the marathon.

3. He came............... home quite late, but he had a good reason.

4. I came .... some old friends at the party.

5. The price of oil is coming ...., so demand will go up.

6. She is trying to come .... the medication but she has to do it gradually.

7. They came .... to Coventry last Christmas, so we've got to go over to theirs this year.

Exercise 2:

Complete the phrasal verb for each sentence. Use the glossary in this unit if you need to.

1. I .... a lot of money when I turned 18 because I inherited it from my grandparents.

2. Now I remember! It's all .... to me.

3. The truth .... when one of the witnesses spoke to reporters and it was published in the press.

4. We need to .... with some creative ideas for the new story. It should be an action thriller with a strong main character.

Answers:

Exercise 1

1. *Mary comes from Ireland and she was born in Dublin.*
2. *Jason came in last in the marathon.*
3. *He came back home quite late, but he had a good reason.*
4. *I came across some old friends at the party.*
5. *The price of oil is coming down, so demand will go up.*
6. *She is trying to come off the medication but she has to do it gradually.*
7. *They came over to Coventry last Christmas, so we´ve got to go over to theirs this year.*

Exercise 2

1. *Came into*
2. *Coming back*
3. *Came out*
4. *Come up*

CHAPTER 17. BONUS CHAPTER: FORMAL VS INFORMAL LANGUAGE

SIX Quick Rules of Formal VS Informal:

1. We tend to understate our feelings and would say I was rather disappointed or I was somewhat surprised instead of saying how we really felt.

2. For the same reason, we do not use exclamation marks.

3. We often use the passive to emphasize the action when the person is of less importance

4. We avoid contractions in formal letters.

5. We use formal equivalence of idiomatic language and phrasal verbs

6. Particular sentence structures can be used to create a formal tone. Inversion is one example of this "Although we were offered an alternative dish, when it was delivered to the table it was cold again".

Exercise 1:

Rewrite the following sentences using formal equivalents for the phrasal verbs. Use a dictionary if necessary. You might need to make other changes to the structures.

1) I'm so chuffed that you've been talked into coming to the meeting.

....

....

2) The football club's facilities have been done up, so this should make our performances better.

....

....

3) As our town is quite cut off, perhaps we could arrange for you to be put up in a hotel in the city for a few days.

....

....

4) We will make up for the inconvenience of having to wait for so long.

....

....

Answers:

1) I am very happy that you have been convinced to attend the meeting.

2) The football club's facilities have been refurbished, which should improve our performances.

3) As our town is quite isolated, we could arrange hotel accommodation in the city for a few days.

4) We will compensate you for the inconvenience of having to wait for so long.

6 Quick Rules of Formal VS Informal:

1. We tend to understate our feelings and would say *I was rather disappointed,* or *I was somewhat surprised* instead of saying how we really felt.

2. For the same reason, we do not use exclamation marks.

3. We often use the passive to emphasize the action when the person is of less importance

4. We avoid contractions in formal letters.

5. We use formal equivalence of idiomatic language and phrasal verbs

6. Particular sentence structures can be used to create a formal tone. Inversion is one example of this *"Although we were offered an alternative dish, when it was delivered to the table it was cold again".*

FORMAL VS INFORMAL LANGUAGE LIST:

It is vital that you can distinguish between formal and informal language in English, not only for this exam, but also for communication in general. Writing a letter or email to a friend is obviously not the same as writing a letter of recommendation for a friend who has applied for a job. Here are some examples of formal and informal words with the same meaning,

VERBS:

FORMAL: INFORMAL

to depart: to go

to carry out: to do

to provide: to give

to retain: keep

to cease: stop

to seek: look for

assist, aid: to help

liberate: to free

obtain: to get

to desire: want

request: to ask for

to function: work

208

to demonstrate: show

to reside: live

require: need

OTHER WORDS:

FORMAL: INFORMAL

subsequently: next / later

immature, infantile: childish

sufficient: enough

further: more (information)

hence, therefore: so

deficiency, lack of: little, there is no

perspiration: sweat

inexpensive: cheap

⁇

LINKING WORDS

LINKING MARKERS

	Openers	Conjunctions	
	Co-ordinating	**Subordinating**	
ADDITION	In addition [to NP], ...	...and ...	, who...
	Moreover, ...	not only ...,	, which...
	Also, ...	but also ...	, where...
	Apart from [NP], ...		, when...
	Furthermore, ...		
CONTRAST	However, ...	... but ...	although...
	Nevertheless, ...	...(and) yet...	whereas...
	On the other hand, ...		while...
	In contrast, ...		in spite of the fact tha
	In spite of [NP], ...		despite the fact that...
	Despite [NP], ...		
CAUSE/	So...	...(and) so...	so...
EFFECT	As a result...	...(and) hence...	so that...
	Consequently...		because...
	Therefore...		due to the fact that...
	Thus...		
	Hence...		
	For this reason...		
	Because of [NP],...		
POSITIVE	In that case,...	...and...	if...
CONDITION	If so,...	...and (then)...	as/so long as...

Note: [NP] = Noun Phrase, which may include a noun, or a verbal noun (-ing form):

e.g. Instead of complaints, it would be better to offer advice

Instead of complaining,...

Exercise 1

Rewrite the information below in 3 or 4 sentences. You must decide how the ideas are logically related and then use a marker or conjunction (coordinating or subordinating) to match your meaning.

Learning French is not easy. Many people would argue that learning Spanish is harder.

French and English share a lot of similarities in their vocabulary. French and Spanish both have different articles for masculine and feminine nouns. You have to change the endings of adjectives to match the nouns. This is hard for speakers of English. English does not use adjective endings.

Most people believe that speaking English helps you to start learning French and Spanish. When you have passed the basic stages, English is less helpful. At an advanced level of Spanish and French, knowing English is arguably not very helpful.

Answers:

Learning French is not easy, but many people would argue that learning Spanish is harder, because French and English share a lot of similarities in their vocabulary. Nevertheless, French and Spanish both have different articles for masculine and feminine nouns. Therefore, you have to change the endings of adjectives to match the nouns, which is hard for speakers of English since English does not use adjective endings. Most people believe that speaking English helps you to start learning French and Spanish but when you have passed the basic stages, English is less helpful and at an advanced level of Spanish and French, knowing English is arguably not very helpful.

Bonus. Free Websites for English Practice

Reading

Links	Descriptions / Instructions
www.breakingnewsenglish.com/	News articles. Full lesson plans, including speaking and listening. GREAT EXERCISES! DO THE LESSON WITH A PARTNER!
http://esl.about.com/od	Various articles and resources with activities. Under **Categories** choose **Advanced English**. Under **Subtopics** choose **Advanced Reading Skills**. Select one of the **Articles &**

Resources that interests you.

Links	Descriptions / Instructions
www.5minuteenglish.com/reading.htm	International Women's Day • Night Study in Korea
www.bbc.co.uk	The news in English. NO EXERCISES.
www.cnn.com/	The news in English. NO EXERCISES.

Grammar

Links	Descriptions / Instructions

214

Links	Descriptions / Instructions
www.englishlearner.com/tests/test.html	Various grammar and vocabulary exercises. Do **Upper Intermediate** and **Advanced** sections.

Listening

Links	Descriptions / Instructions
www.elllo.org/	Listen to the **Audio Archives (001-751+)** and answer the questions.
www.elllo.org/english/Points.htm	Short lectures with test-type questions.
www.esl-lab.com/	Listen to conversations from the **Difficult** section of the **General Listening Quizzes**. Listen to recordings from the **Medium** and **Difficult**

sections of the **Listening Quizzes for Academic Purposes** (EXAM-TYPE QUESTIONS).

Take dictation from the Upper-Intermediate and Advanced listenings.

Includes punctuation vocabulary.

YOU NEED A PEN AND SOME PAPER.

www.dictationsonline.com/

Research and Writing

Links	Descriptions / Instructions
https://www.flo-joe.co.uk	Some good examples of writing corrections although be careful with errors on the

Links	Descriptions / Instructions
www.plainenglish.co.uk/proofreading.pdf	website and inaccurate questions. Proofreading – 10 ways to make your writing better.

Study Skills

Links	Descriptions / Instructions
www.how-to-study.com	Tips on studying effectively.

Pronunciation

Links	Descriptions / Instructions
www.shiporsheep.com/	Hear and practise similar sounds.
www.fonetiks.org/engsou5.html	Hear and practise similar consonants.
www.fonetiks.org/nameseng.html	Hear and practise English names.
www.fonetiks.org/difficult.html	Hear and practise difficult words.

217

www.howjsay.com/	A pronunciation dictionary.
www.spokenenglish.org/	Hear the pronunciation of various English grammar points.
www.foniks.org	Hear and practise sounds.

IELTS SPEAKING PHRASES (BANDS 8.0-9.0)

Likes/dislikes	Opinion
I'm into...	As far as I'm concerned,
I'm a keen/avid (surfer)	As I see it,
I'm keen on/fond of (surfing)	From my point of view,
I (go surfing) to unwind, to	In my humble opinion,
escape the stresses and strains	I'd say that...
of my day to day life.	
I like nothing more than (to go	
surfing)	
I'm itching to try/go.... (I really	
want to)	
Agreeing	**Disagreeing**
We see eye to eye.	We don't see eye to eye.
Yeah, I'd go along with that.	I take your point but...
Absolutely!	I tend to disagree with
You took the words right out	you there.
of my mouth.	That's not always the
I couldn't agree more.	case
You have a point there.	I beg to differ
I'm with you 100% on this one.	Isn't it more a case of...
Starting to make a conclusion	**Asking for opinion**
	What's your take on....?
Let's get down to the nitty	Where do you stand
gritty.	on....?
The bottom line is we have to	In my opinion...., would
choose one...	you go along with that?
It's a tough one, I'm torn	What are your thoughts
between ... and	on this?
Shall we go with ....?	
Personalising	**Impressive structures**
Speaking from personal	Another point I'd like to

experience,... For me personally,.. This is a topic that is particularly close to my heart... It's funny I was just thinking about this the other day. My gut/initial reaction is... If I were to choose one of these situations (part 2 pictures), I'd go with... because...	add about ... is... It's also worth bearing in mind that... Coming back to what (Javi) was saying about .... I'd also like to point out that... I think it's important not to forget that... The vast majority of people tend to think that... At the end of the day... When all's said and done...
Tips Eye-contact Active listening Open body language Speak up Don't dominate	**Asking for repetition** I beg your pardon, I didn't catch that. Sorry would you mind repeating that? Could you repeat the question please?

CHAPTER 19. HOW TO LEARN THOUSANDS OF WORDS IN ENGLISH IN ONLY 6 MONTHS

Do you spend a lot of time and effort in learning vocabulary but still find difficulty using it when required? Have you spent a lot of time memorizing vocabulary words but forget them when you need them the most? Don't worry if you answered a big resounding "YES" to any of these questions because you are not alone. There are a number of useful tools, methods, and exercises which will have you not only remembering, but using your extended vocabulary with minimal effort. Let's get started!

Use Mnemonic Devices

What are mnemonic devices? Well they include a variety of techniques and methods that help remember or recall information.

FANBOYS

For example, many students often need to recall the conjunctions used in English grammar. Remembering FANBOYS is a good tool to recall these words (For, And, Nor, But, Or, Yet, So). The best part of this is you can use your creativity to make it interesting and different. You could create a song out of the words, similar to what many children

221

do when they learn names of countries and capitals. Finding some words that rhyme together would give your song some rhythm, so get creative and don't be afraid to try something a bit silly. Silly is good because it helps the brain remember.

Tongue twisters

Tongue twisters are a fun way of practicing sounds, and this repetition of sounds creates another type of rhythm: *Silly Sally sat by the seashore collecting seashells.*

This can be done with words that begin with the same sound or even have similar sounds within or at the end of a word. It can create an interesting beat or jingle which helps you remember easily and quickly.

Teach it to the mirror!

One of the best and easiest ways to remember anything is to teach someone else. If you can't teach someone else, then teach yourself in the mirror!

Share your knowledge. In order to teach vocabulary to someone else, you need to have a good grasp of the word and the many contexts in which it is used. In fact, if you refer to a dictionary you may find that there are multiple definitions related to the word itself. Before teaching, it's important to study and thoroughly understand the word first. Look for sentences that contain that word so you can understand how it can be used with other words for meaning. Practice making your own sentences as well. Encourage the "student" to ask questions for understanding and clarity.

Make it a part of your daily routine

Now it's important to use what you have learned. As the saying goes: "If you don't use it, you lose it." The first step here is to look for ways to use the new words.

Notecards or post-it notes

Notecards or post-it notes are useful as they are handy. You can stick post-its anywhere as a reminder. Just write the name, short definition, or even a sentence as an example. Here's what your notecard could look like:

Impart: to make known

Synonyms: tell, disclose

Sentence: Teachers impart knowledge to their students.

Learn Suffixes

Suffixes are word endings that may change a word's meaning. They can be used to change a word so that it maintains the rules of grammar. Consider the following sentences

It is a tradition in Chinese culture to eat using chopsticks.

The older generation is more traditional than today's youth.

223

The wedding ceremony is traditionally conducted by a priest.

Learning suffixes and how they change words is a useful tool. With the suffix -ally, as in "traditionally", it is understood that we are using an adverb describing an action. The –tion in "tradition" makes it a noun, so it's often placed at the beginning of a sentence. Understanding placement of words will help you make sure sentences are grammatically correct.

Read, Read, and Read!

Today's fast paced lifestyle makes it challenging, if not impossible, to make the time to read. However, tor increasing English vocabulary, it's absolutely essential. Read what you enjoy reading in your own language but read it in English! If you like music, read about music, if you like business, read business!

The 30 minute Rule

The 30 minute Rule states that thirty minutes of pleasurable reading every day will lead to amazing results in your level of English over time. 'Thirty minute readers', people who read for fun for at least 30 minutes per day, tend to have a vast vocabulary. Furthermore, several studies have suggested that the health benefits can be considerable: living longer, increasing IQ, and reducing stress among other perks. Over time, reading regularly can also increase vocabulary and make it easier to utilize these words in practical and functional situations.

Don't worry if you can't find the time in a busy lifestyle to pick up a book to read.

Look for friends or colleagues who enjoy reading. Often times, interacting with bookworms or avid readers will help you pick up vocabulary or new expressions from them. Don't hesitate to ask about anything that is unfamiliar.

Read Newspapers

A newspaper is a very valuable tool that has a wealth of information at your fingertips. Whether it's the paper version or the electronic version, it doesn't matter. Newspapers are a tool which will spark curiosity and encourage you to read more about a variety of topics.

Spend time interacting with expert professionals in various fields if you can.

That doesn't mean you need to spend time at colleges or universities. Expand your field of awareness and interest to connect to those outside your circle of friends and colleagues. You can join various chat forums or groups in social media. Learn new vocabulary and subjects. You will definitely see the difference.

Download a dictionary app

Anyone who wants to improve their vocabulary really must download an app to their phone. It's not at all practical to lug around a dictionary. A dictionary app on a smartphone can be accessed quickly. Also, being familiar with some online tools that give sentence examples using the words in different contexts is extremely useful. Remember that words fit together in sentences based on their meaning, so it's important to always understand the context or surrounding words so that the sentence or expression makes sense.

Record sentences and structures in your notebook, never single words

NEVER write a single word followed by a definition in your notebook! Always add an example sentence and pay attention to the original sentence where you saw this word. English words can often change meanings depending on the prepositions they go with or the type of sentence they are in.

For example:

He was turned away at the door because he was wearing trainers.

Meaning: He was rejected

He turned away when I tried to speak to him because he was very angry.

Meaning: He looked the other way or turned his head towards a different direction so he didn´t have to look at me.

Make it fun!

Learning new English vocabulary words doesn't have to be a chore! Find ways to make it fun, interesting, and rewarding. Download a few gaming apps that focus on building or using vocabulary words. A common one is "Words with Friends" where you get to share and learn new words with your own circle of friends. Try it! You will see the results.

ONE LAST THING...

If you enjoyed this book or found it useful I'd be very grateful if you'd post a short review on Amazon. Your support really does make a difference and I read all the reviews personally so I can get your feedback and make this book even better.

If you'd like to leave a review then all you need to do is click the review link on this book's page on Amazon here:

Thanks for reading and thanks again for your support!

BOOK 2

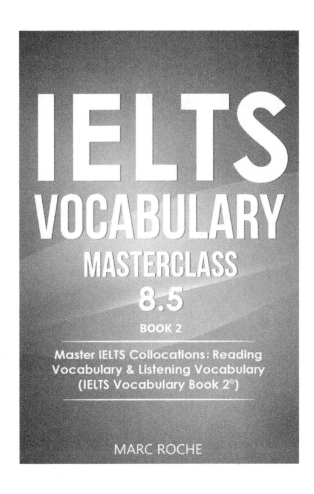

IELTS
VOCABULARY
MASTERCLASS
8.5
BOOK 2

Master IELTS Collocations: Reading
Vocabulary & Listening Vocabulary
(IELTS Vocabulary Book 2®)

MARC ROCHE

IELTS VOCABULARY MASTERCLASS 8.5 ©

BOOK 2

MASTER IELTS COLLOCATIONS: READING VOCABULARY & LISTENING VOCABULARY

IELTS VOCABULARY BOOK 2 ©

MARC ROCHE

8.5

"Your understanding of what you read and hear is, to a very large degree, determined by your vocabulary, so improve your vocabulary daily."

- *Winston Churchill*

Disclaimer

Although the author and publisher have made every effort to ensure that the information in this book was correct at press time, the author and publisher do not assume and hereby disclaim any liability to any party for any loss, damage, or disruption caused by errors or omissions, whether such errors or omissions result from negligence, accident, or any other cause.

Topics covered in this book-

IELTS vocabulary, IELTS listening, IELTS grammar, IELTS speaking, IELTS writing, IELTS reading, IELTS academic, collocations in use

GET MARC ROCHE'S STARTER LIBRARY FOR FREE

Sign up for the no-spam newsletter and get an introductory book and lots more exclusive content, all for free.

Details can be found at the end of the book.

DEDICATION

For my beautiful son, who brightens my day with his smile, his questions and his mischief.

For my parents, who have always been there.

For Maddi, for being such a wonderful mother to my son.

EPIGRAPH

The limits of my language are the limits of my universe.

- *Johann Wolfgang von Goethe*

Vocabulary enables us to interpret and to express. If you have a limited vocabulary, you will also have a limited vision and a limited future.

- *Jim Rohn*

FOREWORD

Dear reader,

Congratulations, you now have a secret pocket-guide with the most important collocations in the IELTS reading and listening tests. You can whip this nifty guide out whenever you want for some quick high-focus revision!

I've been lucky enough to be able to help many students improve their IELTS vocabulary, IELTS listening, IELTS speaking and IELTS Reading & Writing skills over the last ten years or so.

When I first started working as a business writing coach and IELTS teacher in 2009, I felt like I had a lot to learn, and fortunately I still do.

The information in this book comes from hundreds of hours of research and from my practical experience of preparing thousands of students for this exam.

The contents of this book are not exhaustive, but I've tried my best to compile the most original and valuable information possible for you.

Best Regards,

Marc

WHY COLLOCATIONS IN USE?

IELTS Vocabulary Book 2: "IELTS Vocabulary Masterclass 8.5. BOOK 2: Master IELTS Collocations: Reading Vocabulary & Listening Vocabulary"

The reason why IELTS Vocabulary Book 2 focuses exclusively on collocations in use:

Many candidates preparing for IELTS, study countless hours learning hundreds of obscure high-level words, but they never realize something VERY IMPORTANT.

+ The IELTS test is designed so that high-level vocabulary is usually not central to the information being transmitted. This means that you don't need to know most of these words for the exam, you ONLY need to learn how to understand the general message based on the context.

+ IELTS is designed to test your REAL ability in English and collocations are a BIG part of this, so they are VERY common in the reading and listening parts of the exam.

+ Collocations are usually PACKED with meaning and this is why native speakers use them so often in REAL English.

+ BECAUSE collocations are full of meaning, it's often extremely difficult to understand them from context, so you must learn them for the exam.

+ When the IELTS EXAMINERS write the exam, they use collocations to test your REAL ability to understand English.

+ If you want to get a higher band score in the IELTS test, instead of focusing on obscure high-level language, you need to focus on what the EXAMINERS are focusing on! – If the use of collocations is one of the elements they are focusing on, you should learn them.

ABOUT THIS BOOK

**About "IELTS Vocabulary Masterclass 8.5. BOOK 2:
Master IELTS Collocations: Reading Vocabulary &
Listening Vocabulary"**

Listening vocabulary and reading vocabulary are not only
vital if you want to achieve the highest band scores in the
IELTS test, but also if you want to be able to function in
English at an academic and professional level. Master English
collocations in use quickly with this IELTS vocabulary book
packed FULL of highly focused and easy to follow exercises
and explanations. "IELTS Vocabulary Masterclass 8.5. BOOK
2: Master IELTS Collocations" will guide you step-by-step
through ADVANCED level IELTS collocations in use, with
SPECIALISED exercises and review notes for the exam.

"IELTS Vocabulary Masterclass 8.5. BOOK 2: Master IELTS
Collocations", is specially designed for serious IELTS
candidates who don't want to waste time. This vocabulary
book will make you more efficient at learning new terms and
reduce your preparation time, which will give you more free
time to focus on other areas.

Hard work and organization are all it takes when it comes to
the exam. I'd like to wish you the best of luck.

Stay organised, stay focused and stay positive.

HOW TO USE THIS BOOK

"IELTS Vocabulary Masterclass 8.5. BOOK 2. Master IELTS Collocations: Reading Vocabulary & Listening Vocabulary" is designed to help you improve your IELTS vocabulary with a special focus on English collocations. I've written this book for quick reference, as I wanted to avoid it becoming too heavy and theoretical.

The collocations are organized alphabetically into sections for quick reference. Each term includes an explanation of its meaning and an example. At the end of each section you can complete a short review exercise to test your knowledge.

This is not an exhaustive list of collocations that could come up in the IELTS exam, it's more of a curated list of the most common ones in the exam, with a special focus on those that appear in the listening and reading exams.

About The Author

Marc is originally from Manchester and currently lives in Spain. He is a writer, teacher, trainer, and entrepreneur. He has collaborated with organizations such as the British Council, the Royal Melbourne Institute of Technology and University of Technology Sydney among others. Marc has also worked with multinationals such as Nike, GlaxoSmithKline or Bolsas y Mercados.

Learn more about Marc at amazon.com/author/marcroche

OTHER BOOKS BY MARC ROCHE

IELTS Vocabulary Masterclass 8.5 (BOOK 1)

IELTS Writing Masterclass 8.5

Grammar for IELTS 8.5 (Book 1)

IELTS COLLOCATIONS FOR 8.5 (READING & LISTENING VOCABULARY)

Set 1

about time-

This phrase is used to express an event that should have already happened. When it finally happens, someone might say 'it's about time' meaning that they are displeased with how long this event took to occur.

above average -

When something is better than the usual.

absolutely necessary-

Something which is essential.

action movie-

A film centred around exciting sequences of fighting, explosions, or chase scenes.

after dark-

Literally when the sun goes and there is no more sunlight.
Night-time.

after hours-

Use this phrase to talk about things that happen after
normal operating hours of a business or office. It can also
be used to refer to a club or bar that is open later than
others.

after party-

A celebration, usually at a smaller place with less people,
following a bigger celebration.

afraid of-

Used to talk about things that scare you or that you fear.

Pronoun + *verb 'to be' + afraid not-

This is used to express a negative answer regretfully. It can

be used as a gentle way to say that something can't be done

or that something hasn't been done

Question: 'Did Jim finish the project in time?'

Answer: 'I'm afraid not'

against the law-

an action which has been outlawed by the legal system.

alternative medicine-

Holistic medicine which is often natural and traditional.

This type of medicine is 'alternative' to what is often called

western medicine, which usually involves surgeries and

pharmaceutical medications. Another term for alternative

medicine is eastern medicine as many of these practices

come from Asian countries.

alphabetical order-

A way to organize lists of information which follows the same organization as the alphabet by the first letter of the word.

all in-

To be completely invested in something. This can be used to talk about emotional investment as well as financial investment.

all of the time-

Things that happen 'all of the time' happen frequently or continuously.

all over-

When something is finished or completed

amazed by-

When something causes someone to be in awe or feel

shock. This phrase can be used to react to both positive and

negative things.

angry about-

To be mad about something.

apply for a job-

Alerting a prospective employer about your interest in

working for them by submitting an application or CV

(resume).

ask about-

Requesting information about someone or something.

ask for directions-

If a person is lost or unsure about where to go or what to do they may ask for help in order to find their destination.

ask (for) permission-

To request if it is possible to do something from a person in authority over you.

associated with-

To be connected to a person or organization.

Quick Review

Test your knowledge- put the correct collocation in the blank. You might need to change the form of the words.

1. After having two bad interviews, Clara was nervous about_____.

2. That restaurant is great! We go there_____.

3. She has to kill all the spiders in the house because her son is _____them.

4. If you want to succeed in your exams, you have to be _____. It requires constant dedication and hard work.

5. She received a raise due to her _____ performance.

6. You have to _____ if you want to leave work early.

Key:

1. applying for a job

2. all the time

3. afraid of

4. all in

5. above average

6. ask for permission

Set 2

baggage claim-

The place in the airport where one can retrieve baggage that was stowed in the bottom of the plane.

back road(s)-

Opposite of large, busy motorways (highways). These are smaller streets, often in more rural areas, which people may opt to take for less traffic or for a more scenic route.

back pay-

The difference between what an employee is owed and what their employer has actually plaid them. Late payments are examples of back pay.

bad manners-

Social behaviour which is not accepted because it is considered rude.

become unhinged-

Used to speak about someone who is angry or upset to the point of being mentally unstable. This could be for a short period or for a longer period of time.

be someone/somebody-

An important person who has name recognition or other measure of influence.

best practices-

Methods that are considered the most appropriate or efficient ways to complete a task within an industry.

best wishes-

A polite expression used to end written correspondence.

big day-

Another way to describe a meaningful event on a certain

day or a meaningful day. Weddings and other large

ceremonies could be considered big days.

the big picture-

The entirety of a situation. Rather than focus on smaller

finer details, the big picture refers to the overall and

broader perspective of something.

black coffee-

Coffee without milk (or cream in the US) and also usually

without sugar.

a black eye-

A bruising or darkening around the eye after being hit by someone or something.

black ice-

Frozen water on the street or pavement that is particularly dangerous because of how slippery it is and the fact that it's harder to see.

black list-

A group of people who have been deemed unworthy or unfit to work with. This is not usually a real list, but rather people who are for some reason considered undesirable within an industry.

black market-

Buying or selling things illegally. This does not refer to an actual market and does not have a physical place.

black sheep-

Someone who does not fit in with a larger group (like a family) because of differences in behaviour, interest, or opinion.

black tie-

One of the most formal dress codes reserved for very important events that occur in the evening.

blue sky-

Literally a sky without clouds. It can also denote when there is sun or very nice weather.

bode well-

When something bodes well, it is a good or auspicious sign.

book a hotel-

To reserve a room in advanced at a hotel.

break a promise-

To not uphold something that a person said that they would do.

bouquet of flowers-

A unit of flowers usually arranged for decorative purposes.

bounce ideas off each other-

To openly exchange thoughts and opinions with others, often used in problem-solving or brainstorming session.

build a fire-

To make a fire for cooking or warmth purposes.

Quick Review

Test your knowledge- put the correct collocation in the blank. You might need to change the form of the words.

1. The woman was so excited about her _____ that she couldn't sleep the night before. (Her wedding started at 2pm).

2. The new hiree was very experienced so he already knew the marketing _____ .

3. I trust her a lot because she has never _____ to me.

4. She bought an elegant evening dress for the _____ event.

5. He waited for 10 minutes in _____ before he saw his bag on the carousel.

6. I prefer to take the _____ on road trips because they are

always more scenic.

Key:

1. big day

2. best practices

3. broken a promise

4. black tie

5. baggage claim

6. back roads

SET 3

call a cab *(British and Australian)-

Request a taxi for a ride either by phone or with an

application like Uber.

call home-

To use a phone to contact your parents or other close

relations. Used especially when people are not in the same

city.

call in sick-

To contact your employers to let them know about your

absence due to illness.

can do-

This phrase is used as an affirmative answer to a question.

It's like saying 'yes I can', or 'I can do that'. It can also be used as an adjective to describe a person's attitude or

personality.

can opener-

A tool used to open food in a tin. It is sometimes powered

by hand, but it can also be electrical.

canned food (tinned food)-

Food that comes in an aluminium tin, usually vegetables or

fruits.

cast a vote-

Make an official choice for a candidate or party during an

election.

catch a cold-

When someone becomes sick with symptoms of

congestion, headache, and sometimes a fever.

catch the train-

To get on or board a train.

cause a scene/commotion-

To draw attention to oneself in public, usually by speaking

loudly or disrupting the normal state of affairs.

checked baggage-

Bags that are too large to be carried onto a plane and are

stored under the plane during travel.

cocktail party-

Usually a small intimate party held in the evening where alcoholic drinks and sometimes food are served.

come back-

To return to a place you have previously been.

come clean-

To admit to doing something, usually a type of wrongdoing.

come first-

This phrase is used to describe something that is a priority or holds a position of importance.

come in (colour)-

Usually used to describe products that are available in multiple colours or patterns. 'This shirt comes in blue, green and black'

come to mind-

To think of something. When something comes to mind, it means that the idea appeared in your mind.

come true-

When something that someone has wanted to happen for a long time finally happens. Often used with dreams or wishes.

comfort food-

Food that is very filling and makes one feel cosy. It is often food from one's childhood.

(in the) coming weeks/months/years-

This phrase is used to talk about things that are expected to happen in the future.

commit a crime-

To do something illegal.

common interest-

Shared passions or ideas people may have with each other.

conduct research-

To carry out scientific experiments.

convenience store (corner shop)-

A shop which sells a multitude of useful items and

foodstuffs, like snacks, drinks, cleaning and hygiene

products.

copy and paste-

Mostly used for computers and smart phones, this process

involves duplicating text or images so that they can be used

elsewhere on the device.

cookie jar-

A container, usually ceramic, used to store cookies or

similar types of sweets.

creative license-

The freedom someone might take in retelling a story to

make it more interesting to the listeners.

274

current events/affairs-

News stories of note and interest.

cutting edge-

Used to describe the newest and latest technology available.

Quick Review

Test your knowledge- put the correct collocation in the blank. You might need to change the form of the words.

1. They got along very well because of their _____ in stamp collecting.

2. The sweater _____ in four colours.

3. I didn't go to work because I _____ over the weekend.

4. She has a very _____ attitude. She's very positive and resilient.

5. Instead of taking the bus, we decided to _____.

6. My office is throwing a _____ if you would like to join me.

Key:

1. common interest

2. came in (or 'comes in')

3. caught a cold

4. can do

5. call a cab

6. cocktail party

Set 4

a day off-

A day when someone does not go to work or school. This can be because of a holiday or an individual choice to not go to work. Usually this phrase is not applied to Saturdays and Sundays, however, it can be used to describe scheduled days in which one does not work.

deal with someone/something-

To acknowledge a problematic situation, problem, or person and solve the issue. To successfully handle a problem.

dead battery-

Used to describe electronics which have no charge and will not function until the charge is restored, usually used for phones and laptops.

278

deck of cards-

A complete unit of cards for playing games. In games like poker, a standard deck of cards is 54. In games like Uno, a complete deck would be a different number.

in the deep end-

This has two meanings. The literal meaning is the area of a swimming pool with the greatest depth.

The figurative meaning is when someone finds himself or herself in the most complex and complicated part of a problem or situation. If a company throw you in at the deep end when you start a new job, it means that they put you in the job without the necessary training or resources and you are supposed to adapt and learn while you're working.

deep sleep-

Used to describe a period of sleep that was not interrupted by anything.

deep thought-

An idea which is considered particularly profound. It can also be used to describe someone who is thinking about something very intensely. IN this case, we would say something like 'He was in deep thought (He was deep in thought), when suddenly the phone rang'

dining room-

A room in a person's home which is dedicated to eating meals, usually for more formal occasions. A dining room is also the space in which people eat in restaurants.

draw heavily from-

When someone is very influenced by someone or something else. We would say something like 'he draws heavily from other crime novels in his latest book'

draw pictures-

To create a piece of art or other type of visual representation of something, usually with your hands.

draw someone's attention to something-

To purposefully make someone focus on something specific.

do chores/housework-

Complete tasks like tidying, cleaning, organizing around a person's home etc.

do someone a favour-

To do something nice for someone else without expectation of repayment.

do better/worse-

To improve performance at a task. The opposite is for a decline in performance.

do homework-

To complete assignments meant to be finished outside the classroom.

do laundry-

To wash clothing, linens, or other fabric-based materials.

do someone's hair/makeup/nails-

These actions are all used to describe enhancing one's

appearance surrounding these specific attributes.

do someone's best-

When someone attempts to perform a task to the best of

their abilities. It's important to do your best in class if you

want to be successful in the exam.

do someone's part-

To contribute with effort or hard work in a group or team

setting to achieve a specific goal.

do the math-

To make specific calculations, usually used to talk about

money or finances.

do the right thing-

Choosing to do something which is morally right or just.

do time-

Colloquial. Used to describe when someone has been sentenced to spend time in prison or jail. We would say something like this: 'He did time for robbery'.

domestic dispute-

A fight, either verbal or physical, between people who live together.

due date-

A day or time when an assignment or project should be submitted. Also used to describe the date when a pregnant woman's child is predicted to be born.

dye someone's hair/clothes-

To change the colour of someone's hair or clothing using dyes specifically meant for this purpose.

Quick Review

Test your knowledge- put the correct collocation in the blank. You might need to change the form of the words.

1. She was unable to _____ her busy schedule because she had too many meetings and appointments.

2. He always ____ on the weekends when he wasn't working.

3. Hairdressers rarely have the same _____ as they work usually work on the weekends.

4. As children, they almost never ate in the _____ except at Christmas and other holidays.

5. It was clear that the artist ____ from the works of Monet and Degas.

6. I need to _____because I don't have any clean socks.

Key:

1. deal with

2. did housework

3. days off

4. dining room

5. drew heavily

6. do laundry

SET 5

early adopter/adoptee-

The first people to accept something, usually new

technology or ideas.

early bird-

Someone who arrives before an appointed time or very

promptly.

early days-

At the beginning of a project or undertaking before one can

say if it will be successful.

(to have an) early night-

To go to bed sooner than usual.

earn a living/salary (make a living)-

To make enough money to live from your job.

easy access-

A place which is simple to enter or something which is easy to get to.

easy money-

Money that was not difficult to make.

eat in/out-

Eating out refers to eating meals at restaurants or other public establishments, while 'eating in' refers to having a meal in your home or someone else's.

eat well-

This has two meanings: either to eat food that is healthy and nutritious or to eat a large amount of food.

eating habits-

Dietary tendencies.

electric car-

A car that runs at least partially on electric energy rather than petrol.

elevator pitch-

A short speech used to convince someone of something.

empty promise-

A promise which has no hope of being upheld or fulfilled.

entry-level job (position)-

A job which doesn't require much experience. These jobs
are usually reserved for those just beginning their careers.

ethnic group-

People who share a common background, ancestry, or
religion.

even number-

A number which is divisible by two.

evening gown-

A dress worn to formal events. They are usually floor-
length.

evenly distribute-

To uniformly disperse over an area, or to share things

equally amongst people.

evenly matched-

Used to describe people or things that are of equal skill,

talent or quality.

exact likeness-

When two things are almost identical.

exceed expectation(s)-

When someone or something performs better than was

predicted or expected.

existential crisis-

Problems concerning one's belief in their reason for being or purpose in life.

Quick Review

Test your knowledge- put the correct collocation in the blank. You might need to change the form of the words.

1. The family tried to _____ as much as possible as it is healthier.

2. _____ of technology usually remain loyal to the brand.

3. She has the _____ of her mother.

4. Anna left the bar at seven because she wanted an _____.

5. An _____ is very energy efficient.

6. I would even accept an _____; I need the money.

Key:

1. eat in

2. early adopters

3. exact likeness

4. early night

5. electric car

6. entry-level job

SET 6

face a fear-

To find a way to overcome something which scares you.
This often involves people putting themselves in direct
contact with the thing which is causing the fear.

face the facts-

A gentle imperative command asking someone to accept
the difficult reality of a situation.

face wash-

A product which is used to cleanse the face of dirt or
makeup.

fair trade-

This is an economic practice by which international

corporations buy products from the developing world. This
296

particular practice is especially beneficial to the producers as it ensures they will be treated well and not taken advantage of.

familiar face-

Used to describe a person who you have met before, even briefly. It is often used to express pleasure in seeing the other person.

fall asleep-

A verbal expression describing the act of going to sleep.

fall in love-

The process of acquiring profound feelings of attraction for another person.

feed pets-

Giving animals in your care food.

feel free-

Letting people know that they are able to act or do as they please. For example, we could say to a friend who is staying in our house; 'feel free to grab food and drinks from the fridge'

field trip-

Taking students from their normal campus in order to do something educational or fun. These include things like excursions to the theatre, museums, or zoos.

fight fire-

The job of extinguishing fires on a large scale. The person who does this job is called a firefighter.

final destination-

The last place a form of transportation will stop.

finger food-

Light buffet style snacks often served at cocktail parties or before a larger meal.

free time-

A synonym for leisure time. This is used to describe what someone likes doing when they are not studying or working. It's a common theme in the IELTS test.

follow a rule/law-

To behave in accordance to rules and laws.

the following day/month/year-

A time in the future that is yet to come. It just means the day, month or year after what we've mentioned. For example, we could have a dialogue like this:

John - 'Mary, are you working next Friday?'

Mary- 'Yes, why?'

John- 'Could you help me prepare my presentation for the following Monday? I'm feeling quite nervous'

follow your dreams/heart-

To do something that you have always wanted to do. This can be used to describe a career path someone has always wanted to pursue. Following your heart can also be used to reference making decisions using instinct and sentiment rather than logic or reason.

foreign policy-

The laws, legislation, and general dealings that one country has with others.

force of habit-

Things that are done with little thought because someone does them very often.

free fall-

To plummet quickly. This phrase can be used to describe a certain type of rollercoaster which vertically drops riders quickly. It can also be used to when talking about stocks and markets which have lost value unexpectedly fast.

free speech-

The right that an individual has to express their opinions freely through speaking and writing. This includes criticizing one's government or one's employer.

frozen food-

Food that has been frozen in order to preserve it for longer.

frozen solid-

A description of something that is so cold that it has developed ice crystals both outside and in making it seem like one complete mass.

full coverage-

When something is completely covered. This could describe physical objects, or it can be used in a less literal sense. Makeup which completely covers the blemishes could be described as being full coverage. Insurance which provides things like dental and vision could also be described as full coverage.

full house-

A description of a place which has a lot of people. It is most commonly used for homes in which many people are living. It can also be used in poker to describe a particular hand with three cards of the same value and two other cards with the same value.

full length-

When used for physical objects, full length usually means something that reaches to the floor in length, oftentimes dresses and mirrors. It can also be used to describe media like books, TV, and movies which are presented in their entirety.

full moon-

When the entire face of the moon is visible from Earth.

furrowed brow-

The brow is the area between the eyes and hairline.

Furrowing this area means the eyes are usually raised

creating wrinkles in the forehead. It is usually used to

denote when people are thinking or worried about a

problem.

Quick Review

Test your knowledge- put the correct collocation in the blank. You might need to change the form of the words.

1. The _____movie is not shown on airplanes, as it's too long for most short flights.

2. He likes to read sci-fi and horror novels in his _____.

3. Her birthday will be the _____.

4. I usually watch TV before I _____.

5. It was good to see a _____ at the party because I didn't know many people.

6. The children were excited about their _____to the art museum.

Key:

1. full length

2. free time

3. following month

4. fall asleep

5. friendly face

6. field trip

Set 7

gain entry-

To have access to a place and have the ability to go in.

gain weight-

An increase in body mass.

garment bag-

A special bag which is used to store clothing without wrinkles or creases while traveling.

general knowledge-

Knowing a small amount on a wide variety of topics.

get a joke-

To understand the reason why certain things are humorous.

get angry-

To become mad at someone or something.

get dressed-

To put clothes on, usually the clothing one wears to leave

the house.

get hired/fired-

Getting hired means to gain employment. Its opposite is to

'get fired' meaning that someone has been made to leave

their job.

get into trouble-

To do something which will lead to a reprimand or some

other kind of punitive action.

get married/divorced-

To legally wed somebody. The opposite, 'getting divorced' means that a couple has decided to end their marriage.

get paid-

To receive money for doing a job.

get rid of something-

To remove something, usually by putting it in the garbage.

go abroad-

To leave one's country to travel to another. This is usually used for short periods of time like for a vacation.

go crazy-

To lose one's sanity. This can either be said figuratively or literally. In the figurative sense it means to become, and in the literal sense it can mean to go insane.

go for a walk/run-

Walking or running for leisure. This is not usually done as a means of transportation but rather for exercise or pleasure.

go green-

To start practices which are good for the environment. These include things like recycling, composting, or not using more energy than necessary.

go to sleep/bed-

To get into bed and sleep.

go wrong-

When something is amiss and has not happened according to plan.

good cause-

A charitable organization which one can donate money to.

good company-

A group of people who are fun and interesting to be around.

good grade-

Used to describe a positive score on test or other things which are graded.

good looking-

Something which is attractive, this phrase is usually used to describe people, but it can also be used for objects.

good luck-

A phrase used to wish someone success or good fortune. It is often said to people who will soon undergo important events.

give a performance-

To act, sing, dance or complete any other kind of artistic action for an audience.

give someone a hand-

A request for help, usually for a type of manual labour.

give something a go-

To attempt or try something for the first time.

group effort-

People working together to achieve something together.

guilty conscience-

A feeling of regret or remorse that someone has. This is a negative feeling which can usually be relieved after the person has admitted to their wrongdoing.

Quick Review

Test your knowledge- put the correct collocation in the blank. You might need to change the form of the words.

1. Anna wished Eric _____ before he went on his business trip.

2. I will give you the money when I _____on Friday.

3. The little girl was very proud of her _____ in school.

4. The company has decided to _____ in order to seem more eco-conscious.

5. You have to interview before you can _____ at a company.

6. I need to _____ a lot of clothing that doesn't fit anymore.

Key

1. good luck

2. get paid

3. good grades

4. go green

5. get hired

6. get rid of

Set 8

hail a cab-

To hold up one's arm to get a taxi cab to stop for you. This always done on the street. Taxi stands involve queuing and waiting for a taxi to become free.

handle a situation/problem-

To have the capacity to fix an issue.

hang up the phone-

A recall to when phones were in the home and hung from the wall. To hang up the phone means to end a phone call with someone.

happy accident-

A coincidence that ends favourably. This phrase can also be applied to mistakes which lead to unexpectedly good result.

happy ending-

Usually used for stories in TV, books, and films. A happy ending sees all of the main characters' lives having a satisfying conclusion.

happy hour-

Casual events hosted by bars and restaurants which feature discounts on meals and alcoholic drinks for a few hours. Happy hours usually occur early in the evening and were created to attract patrons after work. For this reason, happy hour usually begins at 5pm when many people are finished with work.

hard work-

This phrase can be used in a couple of different ways. It can be used to describe actually difficult physical or mental labour. It can also be used to describe satisfaction with a person's efforts.

haunted house-

An attraction or amusement park that usually happens during Halloween. People walk through a building to be purposefully scared by actors who portray things like ghosts and zombies.

have an allergy/allergies-

When people have a negative bodily reaction to certain foods, plants, animals, or dust. Common reactions include sneezing, red eyes, or an itchy rash. More severe reactions can involve restriction of the airways.

have a meal-

To eat breakfast, lunch, or dinner.

318

have a problem-

To have an issue or other concern which requires attention.

have an idea-

To put forth a thought or opinion about something. This is also a way to express an idea someone is unsure about.

have fun-

To enjoy something or be amused by an activity.

have room-

To have enough physical space for something.

have time-

Having freedom within one's schedule or to be able to do something as your schedule allows.

heavy rain-

Very bad weather, when rain is coming down very hard and fast.

heavy smoker-

A person who has many cigarettes in a day.

heavy traffic-

A time when there are many cars, busses, and other vehicles on the road making for a lot congestion.

hidden agenda-

A secret motive for doing something that is unknown to others.

hidden fees-

Costs which are not usually given up front to someone when buying something. These costs may be related to installation, labour, or commission of a product or service.

high fashion-

A genre of fashion which is marked by luxury, expensive materials, and one-of-a-kind garments.

high score-

Usually in reference to games, a high score refers to the person who has the most points.

high status-

Something which holds a place of extreme importance. This can refer to a person, groups, or organization.

high temperature-

Very hot conditions.

higher education-

Institutions of learning after secondary schools like colleges and universities.

hiring freeze-

A business practice intended to reduce costs by not employing any new people.

hold back-

To refrain from doing something for a time or show restraint.

hold hands-

The act of taking someone else's hands in your own.

hold office-

People who have been appointed or elected to work in politics.

hot sauce-

Any type of spicy condiment which contains chili or peppers.

human error-

When something is the fault of person rather than the fault of the machine or piece of technology that the person is using.

human nature-

Traits and characteristics ascribed to all humans.

Quick Review

Test your knowledge- put the correct collocation in the blank. You might need to change the form of the words.

1. The price nearly doubled after the _____ were taken into account.

2. The _____ caused all of the flowers to wilt.

3. We always take a trip to a _____ for Halloween.

4. Can you _____? I am ready to go home.

5. Donald Trump is the only president who has never _____ before.

Key:

1. hidden fees

2. high temperature

3. haunted house

4. hail a cab

5. held office

SET 9

identity crisis-

A feeling of being uncertain about oneself to the point of

not knowing ones' place in society.

ill effects-

Negative outcomes of something.

ill health-

A period of sickness.

immediate action-

Something that requires attention as soon as possible in

order to divert a problem. This is almost always a negative

thing.

immediate family-

Members of your family who you are the closest with.
They are usually the people you grew up in the same house
with, like your parents and siblings. Your immediate family
can also include family members who live in close
proximity who you see often.

in a row-

Things which form a line horizontally.

in charge of-

To be responsible for someone or something.

in light of-

Decisions or choices made after new information is
learned.

initial stages-

The first steps of a project or process.

an inquiry into-

To seek information about something through official investigation. This is often used to talk about investigations into government, police or army actions and policies.

innocent mistake-

An error that was not made on purpose or intended to harm anyone.

inside joke-

A piece of humour which is based on people sharing an experience. Outside of this context it is not considered funny or requires a lot of explanation.

inside job-

Corruption against a company or industry that is committed by people who are a part of that company or industry.

inspired by-

To be stimulated intellectually or creatively by someone or something.

intelligence agency-

A governmental organization which is in charge of collecting information in order to promote security of the nation.

internal medicine-

The type of medicine practiced by a general doctor.

interest group-

An organization dedicated to promoting their shared interest.

irreparable damage-

Harm which is not able to be fixed.

issue a warning-

To give a formal reprimand after a rule or law has been broken.

Quick Review

Test your knowledge- put the correct collocation in the blank. You might need to change the form of the words.

1. _____ of current events, the company has decided to change their business strategy.

2. I am part of an _____ that advocates for animal rights.

3. The problem with the computer system required _____ from the engineering team.

4. The storm caused _____ to the house.

5. All of the animals stood _____ waiting to be fed.

Key:

1. In light of

2. interest group

3. immediate action

4. irreparable damage

5. in a row

SET 10

job interview-

A meeting held between a prospective job applicant and employer in order to obtain future employment for the applicant.

joint account-

A bank account which is shared by two people.

joint effort-

An accomplishment which is shared by two people

journal entry-

Writings in a personal diary or journal about one particular day in their life.

junk food-

Food that is not healthy and has few benefits to one's body.

This type of food can be as small as a snack or a full meal.

jump to a (the) conclusion- jump to conclusions

When someone believes something unfounded based on

little evidence which actually supports that belief.

junk mail-

Unwanted correspondence. This phrase can be used to

describe physical mail which comes in the post or emails.

Most junk mail is a form of advertisement.

Quick Review

Test your knowledge- put the correct collocation in the blank. You might need to change the form of the words.

1. Don't _____. You don't have enough information about this topic to decide.

2. She is very nervous about her first _____.

3. Too much _____ will ruin your health.

4. If I receive an email I'm not interested in, I usually send it to the _____ folder.

5. Maria and Jack just opened up their own _____ together.

Key:

1. jump to conclusions

2. job interview

3. Junk food

4. junk mail

5. joint account

Set 11

keep a diary-

To maintain an account of your schedule or personal life in a handwritten book.

keep a secret-

Learning confidential information about someone or something and not telling anyone else.

keep busy-

To have a full schedule of activities. This is usually done voluntarily and can include a mix of study, work, and leisure.

keep fit-

To try and maintain a certain level of health by exercising and having a healthy diet.

337

keep going-

To continue in the same direction. This can be an actual physical direction as when someone is driving or walking, or it can mean following a certain plan.

keep the change-

A directive during a monetary transaction. When a bill or coin is more than the amount of a product or good, yet the seller keeps the leftover amount. This is usually done in more casual setting like restaurants.

keep to oneself-

An attempt or desire to not draw attention to oneself.

key part/role-

To have an integral role in creating or developing something.

keynote address/speaker-

A person who is giving a the most important or most anticipated speech at a conference.

knead dough-

To take dough and massage it on a floured surface to incorporate air or stretch it.

knit a sweater-

Taking yarn and needles, especially made for knitting, and using a pattern to create a finished garment.

know about-

Having awareness of something.

know better-

Having the experience and wherewithal to make good

decisions, and yet not making them.

know how-

Particular experience or understand in a certain field or on a

certain topic.

known for-

The reason why someone or something is famous or

important.

keep quiet-

To not make noise or not talk.

keep score-

This has two meaning. Literally, it means to count the points in a game to determine who is winning and losing. Figuratively, it means to track gains and losses between individuals, usually related to personal or professional problems.

kill time-

A purposeful way to waste time.

Quick Review

Test your knowledge- put the correct collocation in the blank. You might need to change the form of the words.

1. The restaurant is _____ its modern Italian food.

2. She tries to _____ by running and biking every day as well as not eating fatty foods.

3. Before we let it rise, we have to _____ for five minutes using extra flour. _

4. I have never been able to _____, I tell my husband everything.

5. Take a left and _____ past the red house on the left.

Key

1. known for

2. keep fit

3. knead the dough

4. keep a secret

5. keep going

Set 12

large scale-

Something that is very big which needs many people or things in order for it work.

last forever-

Something that will never diminish, fade, or lessen in number.

law and order-

The system by which people are governed and follow the rules. This involves the police and the judicial system.

lay groundwork/foundation-

To begin the first steps of a project. These things are often foundational and are the things that must be done before more substantial work can be completed.

344

laugh out loud-

The words behind the popular Internet speak abbreviation of 'lol.' This happens when something is so funny that a person laughs audibly.

lead to believe-

When a person is told information, which makes them think a certain way. This is phrase is often said when contrary information is presented that makes the person doubt their initial thought.

leading role-

The most important part (character) in a play or movie.

let go-

To permit something or someone to leave you.

light a candle-

To put a fire to the wick of a candle until it ignites and

stays alight on its own.

like crazy-

A way to modify an emotion or desire.

live out a dream/fantasy-

To actually fulfil a long-held wish or hope in the way one

imagined.

live performance-

A performance given in real time for an audience.

living room-

A common room in someone's home in which people

gather to relax or work.

lock the door-

To ensure that a door is unable to be opened from the outside.

long term-

Something that will extend far into the future.

look alive-

A command used to tell someone to appear to be busy or seem cheerful.

look forward to-

To anticipate something or be excited about something.

look up information-

To research on a certain topic. This can be done for things like words in a dictionary or general information on the Internet.

lose connection-

When technology which requires a connection to a network in order to work, disconnects from the network and no longer functions.

lose control-

There are two meanings for this collocation: to be unable to maintain poised, usually because of intense emotions. It can also mean to lose being in charge of a situation.

lose faith-

There is a literal and figurative meaning for this collocation. The literal is to no longer believe in religion or a god. The figurative is to no longer have trust in a person, concept, or belief.

lose interest-

To no longer want to do something someone was previously excited about.

lose money-

Companies which are spending more money than they are earning.

lose weight-

To decrease one's body mass.

lose your temper-

To be unable to maintain composure because of strong
feelings of anger.

lose an appetite-

When the desire to eat is no longer appealing. This can also
be used figuratively to describe a situation in which
someone no longer has interest in doing something.

lose your mind-

The loss of sanity.

lose touch with something/someone-

To no longer have contact.

loved one(s)-

Used to describe a person who you feel very close or

attached to, including family members.

Quick Review

Test your knowledge- put the correct collocation in the blank. You might need to change the form of the words.

1. I was _____ that the office would be closed tomorrow.

2. We want to buy a new couch for the _____.

3. Although she used to love painting, she seems to have _____ in it.

4. Christmas is a time to visit _____ in traditionally Christian countries.

5. This watch _____, it never breaks.

Key

1. led to believe

2. living room

3. lost interest

4. loved ones

5. lasts forever

SET 13

make a comeback-

Overcoming a loss and becoming successful again.

make a decision-

To choose one thing over another.

make a fool of oneself-

To do something which makes other people think less of you.

make a fortune-

To earn or win a large amount of money.

make a fuss-

To whine or cause a commotion in order to bring attention to an issue.

354

make a difference-

To cause a positive change in someone's life or for an organization.

make an effort-

To attempt to do the best one can at a job.

make a list-

To write a list of things one wants to remember.

make a meal-

To prepare or cook a meal. This can be used for breakfast, lunch, or dinner.

make a mess-

To leave things in a very disorganized or disorderly fashion.

make a phone call-

To use a phone to contact someone.

make a point-

To put forth ideas in order to persuade others.

make a reservation-

To reserve a place at a restaurant, hotel, or other service with limited space.

make amends-

Apologizing and trying to fix a problem or mistake that harmed another person.

make arrangements-

To organize plans for the future.

make redundant-

To be fired from a job but not due to any fault of your own.

make the bed-

To smooth the sheets and covers of a bed and make it appear neat.

make friends-

To begin an amiable relationship with someone in the hopes of achieving friendship.

make something work-

To fix something which is broken or not working properly.

make money-

The way in which someone earns money.

make light of something-

To behave as is something is not important.

make sense-

A description of something which in coherent and

understandable.

make room-

To empty out an area in a certain space.

manual labour-

Work that can only be completed with a large amount of

physicality, usually not work which is done at an office.

married couple-

Two people who have legally wed each other.

mass market-

Products or good which are produced in huge quantities.

mean well-

To aim to be helpful but not being able to.

minor setback-

A small problem that causes a delay but is not detrimental.

miss a connection-

Used for travel. When change from one plane, train, or bus
to another is necessary, but for some reason the passenger
is unable to make the second mode of transport.

mirror image-

Two things which look exactly the same.

most of the time-

Usually, often, frequently.

more or less-

An approximate or estimate.

money maker-

Something which is very lucrative and brings in money for
a company.

mountain range-

A group of mountains.

Quick Review

Test your knowledge- put the correct collocation in the blank. You might need to change the form of the words.

1. I always _____ as soon as I wake up.

2. Lots of people like her, so it's easy for her to _____.

3. You have to _____ about whether you will stay here or go home for the holiday.

4. _____ would cost a lot of money as you would need to rebook your next flight.

5. Children aren't very neat and tidy, and they tend to

_____.

Key

1. make the bed

2. make friends

3. make a decision

4. missing a connection

5. make a mess

SET 14

nasty habit-

Something that someone does often but that is bad for their health or unpleasant in some way for others.

nasty weather-

Unpleasant weather usually involving storms or extreme temperatures, either hot or cold.

national average-

The norm or typical amount of something for a country.

native language/tongue-

The language someone learns first or the language that they speak most often at home.

native speaker-

Someone who has spoken a particular language since birth or since they were very little children.

natural disaster-

A catastrophe which was not made by man but was rather caused by nature. This includes things like tornadoes, hurricanes, wildfires, or earthquakes.

natural resources-

A reserve which occurred without human intervention. These are often things which humans rely upon or have learned to value such as sunlight, wind, and water.

near death experience-

The experience of almost dying. This could be caused due to an accident or medical event.

near future-

A time to come which will happen soon.

net worth-

The money and all other assets which have monetary value

that a person or company is worth.

nervous about-

To be anxious or concerned about something.

nervous breakdown-

Used to describe someone who is suffering from severe

mental distress to the point of being unable to function.

new and improved-

Usually used to describe products which have undergone changes in order to be made better and more attractive for customers.

newly acquired-

Something which has recently been gained by a company. These acquisitions are usually smaller companies which have been take over by larger companies.

New Year's Eve/Day-

For those using the solar calendar, New Year's Eve is the last day of the year, December 31st. New Year's Day is the first day of the new year, January 1st. New Year's Day is usually a holiday.

next door neighbour

The people who live in the houses near you. This can also be applied to people who live in apartment building. In this case it would be the people who live in the units nearest yours.

next time-

The occurrence of something after this time.

non-stop flight-

A flight on an airplane which does not have any layovers. A non-stop will not land until it has reached its final destination.

nowhere near-

A description of something which is far away from wherever the speaker is currently at.

367

null and void-

Used to speak about a legal document or process which no longer has any legal weight.

nutritional value-

The total amount of vitamins, protein, fat, etc. in food which can affect the body after consumption.

Quick Review

Test your knowledge- put the correct collocation in the blank. You might need to change the form of the words.

1. The field trip was cancelled due to the _____.

2. The contract was made _____ after the company decided not to move forward with the merger.

3. That office is _____ here. You need to drive 30 minutes to get there.

4. My _____ is English, I don't know any other languages.

5. The earthquake was an unprecedented _____. It caused a massive amount of damage.

Key

1. nasty weather

2. null and void

3. nowhere near

4. native language

5. natural disaster

Set 15

occupational hazard-

Dangers related to working at a specific job.

odd number-

Numbers which end in an odd number, the opposite of even numbers.

old age-

Used to describe a person who is elderly.

office job-

A job which is performed mostly at an office.

on time-

Happening at the appointed time.

on TV-

Something which is broadcasted on the television.

operating hours-

The times which a place is usually open for business.

out of time-

When there is not enough time to complete a task.

owe money-

To be obligated to pay someone money which was previously borrowed.

overall effect-

The complete impression something leaves on someone.

overly exaggerated-

Overstating how good or bad something is. *(Completely exaggerated)

Quick Review

Test your knowledge- put the correct collocation in the blank. You might need to change the form of the words.

1. Meetings always start _____ at my office.

2. We've passed the deadline so we're _____.

3. My parents ____ to the bank for the house.

4. The _____ of the painting makes me think of the sea.

5. Back pain is an _____ of construction work.

Key

1. on time

2. out of time

3. owe money

4. overall effect

5. occupational hazard

SET 16

pack a bag-

To place one's belongings in a suitcase or other type of luggage, usually for a trip.

pair of glasses/pants-

Although glasses and pants are singular items, due to having two lenses and two legs, respectively, they are referred to as a pair.

paint someone's nails

To polish fingernails or toenails with a coloured enamel.

pass a law-

When legislation becomes official by a voting governing body.

pass test-

To make a grade which is sufficient enough to constitute a positive exam result.

pathological liar-

A person who lies frequently and habitually without having need to. These lies often make the person who tells them seem more interesting or successful than they actually are.

pay a visit-

To make a special social appointment to see someone.

pay attention-

To give focus to something by observing it closely.

pay day-

The day when someone is scheduled to receive money for

work they have done.

peace and quiet-

Quiet and solitude with no noise.

perfect timing-

Knowing the exact right moment to do something.

personal belongings-

Objects which are the property of someone.

piece of paper-

A sheet of paper.

piece of music-

A composed work of music. This can refer to any genre of music.

play games-

There are two meanings for this phrase. To engage in a friendly competition in which one can win or lose. It can also mean to handle a situation in a non-serious fashion or without respect.

pleasant surprise-

An unexpected situation which has a positive outcome.

point of view-

One's way of thinking or a particular outlook or perspective on something.

popular opinion/belief-

Something which is believed to be true by many people.

post office-

The place where one can send and receive packages or buy boxes and postage for shipping.

prepare for the worst-

To expect that something bad will happen.

press a button-

To depress a key, bell, or ringer in order to achieve something.

prison sentence-

Punishment for committing a crime which involves a stretch of time spent in prison or jail.

pull a muscle

An injury involving stressing or stretching a muscle to the point of pain.

push back-

Either to delay a date or a negative reaction to something.

put on clothes/shoes-

To wear clothing and shoes on the body.

Quick Review

Test your knowledge- put the correct collocation in the blank. You might need to change the form of the words.

1. I like _____ after the noise and stress of work.

2. Please gather all of your _____ before leaving the airplane.

3. She likes to _____ red because it is her favourite colour.

4. I would like to _____ to my aunt because she is in the hospital.

5. The company has received _____ after the controversial news came out.

Key:

1. peace and quiet

2. personal belongings

3. paint her nails

4. pay a visit

5. push back

SET 17

quality control-

The branch of a company which is responsible for ensuring that their products all have the same standard of quality.

quality of life-

The general conditions of how people live in a certain place. It can be described as good, excellent, high, low etc.

quick bite-

Eating food when one does not have a lot of time to devote to sitting down at a restaurant or cooking a meal.

quiet night in-

Spending the night at home.

quit my job-

To leave your job voluntarily.

Quick Review

Test your knowledge- put the correct collocation in the blank. You might need to change the form of the words.

1. I want to get a _____ (to eat) before the movie. I'm starving.

2. The _____ department needs to be alerted because there have been some complaints.

3. I haven't enjoyed working in this company for months, so I might _____.

4. Let's have a _____ and stay at home.

5. Many people want to live here because of the excellent _____.

Key:

1. quick bite

2. quality control

3. quit my job

4. quiet night (in)

5. quality of life

Set 18

rainy day-

To describe a day in which it is raining.

raise concern-

To formally express apprehension about something.

raise your voice-

This phrase has two meanings. It can either mean to express yourself in a more obvious way, or it can mean speaking too loudly.

read aloud-

To read using your voice so that others can hear you. Its opposite is reading to yourself.

receive presents-

To get gifts from someone.

receiving end-

To be affected by the intentional actions of someone else. It is usually not a positive position to be in.

recent graduate-

A person who has just matriculated through an educational institution, usually university.

red eye-

A flight which departs late in the evening and arrives to its destination early in the morning.

regular exercise-

Working out on a consistent schedule.

research and development-

A branch of company which is dedicated to discovering
and exploring new products or areas of interest.

ride a horse-

To sit on a horse for transportation, sport, or leisure while it
walks or runs.

ride a motorcycle/bike-

To use these vehicles for transport or leisure.

rough draft-

A finished form of a written work that still needs further
editing.

royal family-

The monarchy of a country.

running water-

Water which is accessible inside the home through a

system of pipes. Synonymous with indoor plumbing.

runny nose-

Often the symptom of a cold or flu, when the nose has an

uncontrollable flow of mucus.

run late-

Not being able to arrive at an agreed upon time. This is the

opposite of being on time.

rush hour-

Periods of time when traffic on the roads is particularly

heavy because of commuters going to and leaving work.

There are usually two rush hours per day, one in the

morning and one in the afternoon.

Quick Review

Test your knowledge- put the correct collocation in the blank. You might need to change the form of the words.

1. The ____ flight leaves at 9pm.

2. I hate _____ because it is difficult to drive in all the water

3. I wanted to leave early in order to avoid (the) ____ traffic.

4. She _____ to her boss about not making enough money.

5. With _____ and a good diet it is easy to be healthy.

Key:

1. red eye

2. rainy days

3. rush hour

4. raised concerns

5. regular exercise

SET 19

save money-

The opposite of spending. Saving money is an attempt to be
frugal with one's finances.

schedule an appointment-

To arrange to be somewhere at a specific time. This is not
usually used for social engagements, but rather for
business.

scented candles-

A candle that gives off a pleasant smell.

second opinion-

Seeking out the opinion of another person or professional,
usually because one is dissatisfied with the opinion of the
first person they asked.

secret Santa-

A gift-giving game played at Christmas in which a group of people purchase gifts for each other without knowing who will give whom a gift.

see through-

A description of a fabric or other material which is transparent.

set the table-

To place dishes, silverware, napkins, and glasses on a table in preparation for having a meal.

serving size-

The appropriate amount of food to eat in one sitting.

shake hands-

A greeting in which two people grasp hands briefly.

shelf stable-

Used to describe foods or other products like cosmetics which do not need refrigeration to remain fresh.

skip a meal-

Not eating breakfast, lunch, or dinner, either as a way to lose weight or because one does not have time for them.

social life-

The leisure time one spends with friends and family outside of work or studies.

solve a problem/issue-

Talking a series of actions in order to fix a difficulty.

sore throat-

A pain in the throat. This could be due to speaking too much, too loudly, or being ill.

sounds good-

An affirmative answer which confirms that the speaker is happy with the present situation.

square dance-

A type of group dance which involves repetitive steps.

spare room-

This phrase can be used to describe a room in someone's house which does not have an allocated purpose and can be used for visiting guests. This phrase can also be used to speak about any extra space in a location.

speak highly (of someone)-

To say words of praise about someone or something.

special occasion-

A positive event which does not happen often.

spend time-

To allot time to doing a particular activity.

still going-

Something that hasn't stopped yet.

study hard-

To work diligently at learning new material.

Quick Review

Test your knowledge- put the correct collocation in the blank. You might need to change the form of the words.

1. My sister sleeps in the _____when she comes to visit.

2. I have a _____ after speaking all weekend at the conference.

3. She often has to _____ because she can't leave work during the day.

4. The curtains won't protect us from the sun because they're _____.

5. I am cooking more at home in order to _____.

Key

1. spare room

2. sore throat

3. skip lunch

4. see through

5. save money

Set 20

take a photo-

To use a camera to capture photo.

take a survey-

To complete a questionnaire about one's thoughts or

experiences, usually for scientific experiments.

take a test-

To complete an exam.

take a taxi-

To use a taxi to get from one place to another.

take toll-

Something which causes injury or damage (usually slowly

and gradually).
402

take care-

To be careful or focus of your wellbeing.

take in clothing-

Taking clothing to the tailor to make it smaller. The opposite is to let clothing out which makes it bigger.

take off clothes/shoes -

To remove clothing or shoes from the body.

talking head-

News and sports correspondents who speak about their respective fields on television programs.

tell time-

To use a watch in order to know the time.

throw a tantrum-

To scream and yell due to anger or displeasure, usually used to talk about childish or childlike behaviour.

Quick Review

Test your knowledge- put the correct collocation in the blank. You might need to change the form of the words.

1. It is clear that the long hours at work are _____ on her health.

2. My two-year old son is just learning how to _____ using an analogue clock.

3. All of the students at the school must _____ to graduate.

4. The angry patron _____ after the manager refused to help her.

5. I always use my phone's camera to _____.

Key

1. taking a toll

2. tell time

3. take a test

4. threw a tantrum

5. take photos

Set 21

undergo surgery-

To be operated upon for medical purposes.

unfair advantage-

A benefit which is not evenly applied to everyone.

upper management-

The most senior levels of a company or business.

upset about-

To be bothered or agitated about

upset stomach-

To feel pain in the abdomen, indigestion.

used car-

A vehicle which has been owned by someone else.

Quick Review

Test your knowledge- put the correct collocation in the blank. You might need to change the form of the words.

1. After eating too much food, you may have an_____.

2. Buying a _____ is cheaper than buying a new one.

3. I knew she was _____ something because she was crying.

4. Some people view being wealthy as an _____ in life.

5. He had to _____in order to repair his ligament.

Key:

1. upset stomach

2. used car

3. upset about

4. unfair advantage

5. undergo surgery

Set 22

vague memory-

A faint recollection of something that is not fully formed.

vast majority-

Most or many of something.

victory lap-

A way of celebrating after winning a competition. Literally, it means an extra lap around a track after a win. Figuratively, it is any type of celebration after any type of win.

visiting hours-

The times available for people to visit others in the hospital or similar institutions.

voice your opinion-

To express the way you think or feel on a certain topic.

Quick Review

Test your knowledge- put the correct collocation in the blank. You might need to change the form of the words.

1. The hospital's _____ are from 9am to 5pm.

2. She only had a _____ of where she might have lost her keys.

3. It is important to _____ in meetings.

4. The _____ of people spend their free time watching series and chatting on social media.

5. They took a _____ around the bar after they won trivia night.

Key

1. visiting hours

2. vague memory

3. voice your opinion

4. vast majority

5. victory lap

SET 23

walk the dog-

To put a pet dog on a leash and take it outside for exercise

or to let it go to the bathroom.

wake up-

The opposite of going to sleep.

wash clothes (do the washing)-

To clean clothes with soap and water, usually by using a

washing machine.

wash my/your face-

To clean one's face of dirt or makeup using water and some

kind of cleanser.

415

washing machine-

A special machine used to wash clothing mechanically.

waste time-

Not using time in a productive matter. This is usually not done on purpose, but rather on things that someone thinks are useful but actually are not.

wide variety-

A large collection.

wilful ignorance-

Ignoring evidence which is contrary to a person's beliefs so that the person can still maintain that their beliefs are correct.

416

win the lottery-

Getting money after playing the lottery.

wishful thinking-

Imagining a future which is based on one's desires rather than actual evidence.

wise man/woman-

A man or woman who has a lot of wisdom.

within reason-

Something that is an attainable goal.

wrap a present-

To cover a gift in decorative paper before presenting it.

work out-

To exercise.

Quick Review

Test your knowledge- put the correct collocation in the blank. You might need to change the form of the words.

1. My father always _____ early, even on the weekend.

2. If I _____, I would buy a new house.

3. The _____ is broken so my clothes are in the sink.

4. Can you _____ after work? He has been inside all day.

5. She doesn't like to _____ being on social media.

Key

1. wakes up

2. won the lottery

3. washing machine

4. walk the dog

5. waste time

SET 24

yearly review-

An evaluation which happens every year.

yet again-

Something that has re-occurred.

you guys- (American)

A plural version of you.

young man/woman-

A youthful person.

Quick Review

Test your knowledge- put the correct collocation in the blank. You might need to change the form of the words.

1. My friend was late _____, so I left the party without her,

2. Can _____ please bring some snacks?

3. The _____ over there is the one who helped me.

4. Her company's _____ is in April.

Key

1. yet again

2. you guys

3. young man

4. yearly review

THANK YOU

I hope you've found it useful!

As I mentioned in the foreword, a lot of hard work has gone into this project.

My whole objective with this book is to help you reach your ultimate goal of achieving an 8.5 in your IELTS test. As I mentioned at the start, this book is not designed to be an exhaustive list of collocations, but instead, a focused and easy-access guide for exam preparation. Review any sections that you feel you need to and use them as a starting point for further research and practice.

BOOK 3

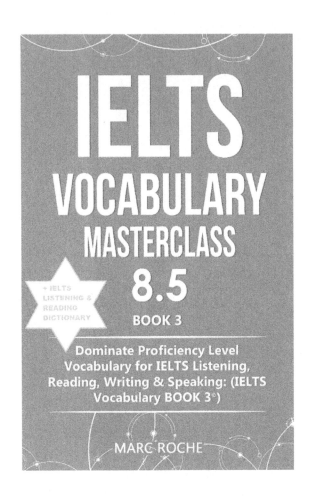

IELTS
VOCABULARY
MASTERCLASS
8.5

+ IELTS
LISTENING &
READING
DICTIONARY

BOOK 3

Dominate Proficiency Level
Vocabulary for IELTS Listening,
Reading, Writing & Speaking: (IELTS
Vocabulary BOOK 3°)

MARC ROCHE

IELTS VOCABULARY MASTERCLASS 8.5 ©

BOOK 3

+ IELTS LISTENING & READING DICTIONARY

DOMINATE PROFICIENCY LEVEL VOCABULARY FOR IELTS LISTENING, READING, WRITING & SPEAKING

IELTS VOCABULARY BOOK 3 ©

MARC ROCHE

8.5

"You can't build up a vocabulary if you never meet any new words. And to meet them you must read."

- *Rudolf Flesch*

Disclaimer

Although the author and publisher have made every effort to ensure that the information in this book was correct at press time, the author and publisher do not assume and hereby disclaim any liability to any party for any loss, damage, or disruption caused by errors or omissions, whether such errors or omissions result from negligence, accident, or any other cause.

Topics covered in this book-

IELTS vocabulary, IELTS listening, IELTS grammar, IELTS speaking, IELTS writing, IELTS reading, IELTS academic, IELTS General Training

GET MARC ROCHE'S STARTER LIBRARY FOR FREE

Sign up for exclusive content via email and get an introductory book and lots more, all for free.

Details can be found at the end of the book.

DEDICATION

For my beautiful son, who brightens my day with his smile, his questions and his mischief.

For my parents, who have always been there.

For Maddi, for being such a wonderful mother to my son.

EPIGRAPH

Your inability to see other possibilities and your lack of vocabulary are your brain's limits, not the universe's.

- Scott Adams

One forgets words as one forgets names. One's vocabulary needs constant fertilizing or it will die.

- Evelyn Waugh

HOW TO USE THIS BOOK

IELTS Vocabulary Masterclass 8.5 © BOOK 3 + IELTS Listening & Reading Dictionary - Dominate Proficiency Level Vocabulary for IELTS Listening, Reading, Writing & Speaking (IELTS VOCABULARY BOOK 3 ©)

The Masterclass to 8.5 is simple:

This book is not designed to be an exhaustive list of words, but instead, a focused and easy-access guide for exam preparation + an IELTS Listening & Reading Mini-Dictionary. Review any sections that you feel you need to and use them as a starting point for further research and practice.

1. Read the definitions and write down an example sentence for each vocabulary item.

2. At the end of each topic chapter, you'll find an exercise to review your understanding of the vocabulary. The examples in the exercises are fragments from IELTS Speaking, IELTS Writing, IELTS Listening and IELTS Reading style questions and answers. After reading the definitions, complete the example sentences, using the words in the chapter.

3. Check your answers.

4. Check your original sentence again and see if it needs corrections.

5. Make clean *Notes / write a definition in your own words and an example sentence in your *Notes.

6. Re-read your *Notes twice per day and practise saying the sentences.

7. There is an IELTS Listening and Reading Mini-Dictionary for quick reference.

8. This is a perfect addition to IELTS Vocabulary 8.5 Masterclass Book 1 & Book 2, but also to the book IELTS Speaking 8.5 Masterclass and IELTS Writing 8.5 Masterclass. Practice answering the speaking activities (speaking cards and exam questions) at the back of the book IELTS Speaking 8.5 Masterclass in front of a mirror or with a partner if possible. When you do this, apply time limits to make it more like the real exam and use language from this book to instantly improve your speaking score!

9. Use the "Blank Notes Section" at the end of this workbook to add your own notes and record your progress.

About The Author

Marc is originally from Manchester and currently lives in Spain. He is a writer, teacher, trainer, and entrepreneur. He has collaborated with organizations such as the British Council, the Royal Melbourne Institute of Technology and University of Technology Sydney among others. Marc has also worked with multinationals such as Nike, GlaxoSmithKline or Bolsas y Mercados.

Learn more about Marc at amazon.com/author/marcroche

OTHER BOOKS BY MARC ROCHE

IELTS Vocabulary Masterclass 8.5 (BOOK 1)

IELTS Vocabulary Masterclass 8.5 (BOOK 2)

IELTS Speaking 8.5 Masterclass

IELTS Writing Masterclass 8.5

Grammar for IELTS 8.5 (Book 1)

IELTS VOCABULARY FOR 8.5: PROFICIENCY VOCABULARY FOR READING, LISTENING, SPEAKING & WRITING SKILLS

TOPIC 1. PEOPLE

Acquaintance= (n) when you know someone well enough to say hello and talk to them when you see them, but they're not a friend.
Sibling = brother or sister
Characteristic = typical
Resemble = when something looks similar to something else, it resembles that thing.
Reliable = something or someone that can be trusted for functional things (something or someone you can rely on).   *Note: the opposite is 'unreliable'
Bond = means a close link or to form a close link if we use it as a verb
Conscious = when your conscious of something it means you're aware of something.
Inherent = a natural part of something is inherent to that thing.
Self-esteem = the level confidence or belief you have in your own abilities and positive qualities.   *Note: Self-esteem is often described as 'high' or 'low'.

Stereotypical = something that fits into the typical ideas about the way it should be.
Tendency = something that happens repeatedly. Trend.
Gender = the sex of a person.
Lifetime = the period of time that something exists or that a person or an animal lives.
Sympathise = when you sympathise with someone it means that you understand their position and situation. It's similar to having empathy.
Hardwired = instinctive behaviour
Habitually = usually

Exercise

Choose a word or phrase from the definitions above and write it in the correct gap below.

- If there is more than one possible answer, choose the best option for the sentence.

- You might need to use the same word or phrase more than once in some cases.

- You may need to adapt the form of the word to fit into the sentence. For example, you might need to change a verb to third person singular to ensure subject-verb agreement like *bond-bonds.*

1. Certain types of bird only live in one place in their entire ....

2. I really .... with all the people who lost their jobs, because nobody wants to be in that situation. I think the government can do more to help them at the moment by doing X, Y and Z for example.

3. I'm .... that I will need to work very hard to become a doctor, but it's my dream and I'm wiling to make the sacrifice.

4. Getting into a car accident is one of the .... dangers of driving, so it's very important that drivers pay full attention on the road so we can minimise the risk.

5. White sharks do not .... attack humans, unless they confuse them with seals. However, they have a really bad reputation, and I think this has contributed to a lot of shark deaths over the years, as they've been actively hunted in many parts of the world.

6. Studies suggest that people with higher .... are more likely to be successful in their careers.

7. I want to study accounting, but I don't think I'm the .... accountant. The stereotypical accountant is a very organised and methodical person who enjoys siting at a desk crunching numbers (making calculations).

8. There is a .... nowadays to socialise through technology. I think it has some very clear benefits, but it

needs to be used in moderation. The benefits are X, Y and Z. However, the dangers are A, B and C.

9. I think our desire to improve and grow is .... into us as humans, but it needs to be stimulated. This is why I strongly believe that we need to promote real-world, practical education. If people see that they can learn real-world skills, it will encourage them to keep learning.

10. In my opinion, ... is sadly still and issue we need to tackle in today's workplace. There are still great disparities between male and female employees in terms of wages and opportunities.

11. I don't know her very well, she's not really a friend, she's more of an ....

12. The shop offers a discount for.................... who sign up for store cards.

13. Adding soy sauce while you're cooking the vegetables gives the dish its .... Vietnamese flavour.

14. Porche's new 2020 car model .... the old 1970s models.

15. It's important for me that my friends are ...., I don't like people who are late or who cancel plans at the last minute.

16. My car is very ...., it has never broken down.

17. I'm very close to my family, we have a very strong ....

18. It's important for people to .... if they work together closely. It's easier to do this in small offices rather than big offices. This is why I prefer working for small companies, as they tend to have a smaller, friendlier environment.

Topic 2. Health & Medicine

Allergic = when you have a negative physical reaction to a substance.

Harmful = not safe, bad for a person or bad for something.

Appetite/hunger = your desire for something (usually food).

*Note: 'crave' means when you really want something. A strong desire for something.

Lifestyle = the way someone lives their life. Your lifestyle can be active, sedentary, sociable, etc…

Ingredients = the components of a specific medicine, drink, food or dish.

Nutritious = full of vitamins, fat, protein, carbohydrates or other essential components for good health.

Suffer = feel discomfort or pain. It can also be used to describe when something negative happens to you or when you have a negative health condition.

Sedentary = the opposite of active. This is often used to describe jobs, activities and lifestyle.
Psychological = related to psychology or the mind.
Beneficial = good, positive or helpful.
Detrimental = bad or negative. Not helpful
Intake = consumption/the amount you eat or drink.
Eradicate = get rid or something (exterminate)
Well-being = your well-being is your level of comfort, health and happiness.
Severity = the seriousness of something.
Preventive = actions that aim to prevent or stop something

Additives = the chemicals that are added to food and drink to stop it from rotting or to enhance favour.

Preservatives = the chemicals that are added to food and drink to keep it fresh for longer.

Administer= to give a patient a medicine or medical treatment.

Admit = to officially allow someone to stay in hospital for medical care.

Agony = intense physical pain or emotional suffering.

Antidote = a drug that stops the negative effects of a poison.

Consultant = an experienced doctor in a hospital who specialises in a specific area of medicine.

Diagnosis = an official conclusion about a patient's condition, given by a doctor.
Inoculate = to use a vaccine protect people against a disease (to vaccinate).
Nursing home (Care home) = a place where the elderly live when they are not able to look after themselves due to their age or due to an illness.

Exercise

Choose a word or phrase from the definitions above and write it in the correct gap below.

- If there is more than one possible answer, choose the best option for the sentence.

- You might need to use the same word or phrase more than once in some cases.

- You may need to adapt the form of the word to fit into the sentence. For example, you might need to change a verb to third person singular to ensure subject-verb agreement like *bond-bonds*.

1. I don't think I could ever work in an office, as I don't think I'd like that .... I'm an active person who enjoys doing things outdoors and moving around a lot and staying in one place indoors for 8-12 hours a day every day is my idea of hell!

2. My uncle was .... with Crohn's disease several years ago, but he still works full-time and hasn't let it stop him from pursuing most of his hobbies.

3. He works as a cardiology .... at a children's hospital in the city centre. His work is very demanding but he's passionate about it.

4. A funny story happened to me on my last birthday. I took my dog to get .... against rabies and someone had brought an abandoned dog into the vet's to try and help it. Long story short, I ended up adopting another dog!

5. If you get bitten by a poisonous snake, it's important to go to hospital so they can give you an ....

6. There has been a lot of controversy surrounding the level of care in some ....

7. When I broke my leg I was in ...., so I rang my friend and she took me to hospital.

8. The more people are .... into hospitals, the higher the demand on medical staff and other resources.

9. The drug is .... orally, twice a day.

10. It's better for your health of you avoid eating too many foods that contain ....

11. It was .... when my team lost the championship in the last 3 seconds of the game! (This is an exaggeration, but very common)

12. Having your heart broken is ....

13. My favourite dish is peperoni pizza. The .... are pizza dough, cheese, tomato, peperoni, olive oil and chilly.

14. Our .... is more important than money. We need to focus on this so that we can eradicate this problem.

15. It's important to monitor your daily .... of trans fats.

16. Too much sugar can be extremely .... to your health.

17. .... medicine is often more effective than treatment. (It aims to stop diseases before they develop)

18. We underestimated the .... of the situation.

19. The government has put .... measures in place so that businesses can recover as quickly as possible.

20. We need to .... the problem now or it will cause more damage in the future.

21. I think junk food increases your ...., as it has very little substance. It doesn't fill you for long and makes you crave more.

22. The .... impact of what has happened has been enormous. It has changed the way we live and the way we view the world.

23. I need to exercise more because I have a very .... job, where I spend most of the day sitting down at a desk.

24. Avocados are very ...., they are packed with iron, vitamins and healthy fat.

25. I .... quite a lot during the lockdown, as I couldn't visit my family.

26. Jack .... a car accident when he was younger, and it changed his life. He is now extremely successful and responsible.

27. People who .... from rare genetic disorders need more guidance from doctors.

28. It would be .... if we could have more telecommuting from now on, as it reduces potential risks and reduces damage to the environment. It is also cheaper for many companies, so everyone would benefit from this type of change.

29. The pandemic has been very .... to businesses all over the world.

30. Smoking is very .... not just to the person smoking, but also to the people around. This is why we need to make it illegal in my opinion.

31. I'm .... to nuts, so I need to be very careful when I eat out in restaurants.

32. I believe that the government needs to introduce tighter restrictions to regulate the .... in natural remedies, as they are often potentially dangerous.

Topic 3. Social & Leisure

Conform = to follow social rules.

Cooperate = when people work well together

Mindset (frame of mind) = the way you think. Your mental attitude at a particular point in your life or in a particular situation.

Minority = a small percentage of a group or population.

Shun = to reject

We can't .... our responsibility as citizens. We have to be sensible and responsible to prevent dangerous situations like this from happening again.

Conventional = the usual, normal or traditional way of doing something or thinking. 'Conventional wisdom' is an expression, meaning: what most people believe to be true, or what most experts accept as the truth.

Interaction = communication between people (written, spoken or through sign language for example).

Pressure = stress or expectations.

Conduct = This can be used as verb and as a noun meaning behaviour-behave. When used as a verb to mean 'behave', it is reflexive, meaning it goes with myself, yourself, himself, herself etc..

Pronunciation *Note: the stress is on the first syllable when it's used as a noun and on the second syllable when used as a verb.

Mainstream = common likes or ideas. Popular

Appropriate = acceptable or suitable for a particular situation.

Multicultural = something that has several different cultures. It can be a team, a department, a city, a country etc..

Absorbing = something that entertains you so much, that you forget about everything else.

Exhilarating = something that makes you feel full of energy and excitement. Thrilling.

Indulge = to do something that you like (like a reward).

Pursue = to follow an activity in order to reach a goal. Think of chasing your dreams.
Tedious = not exciting. Focusing on highly specific but boring things (in the speaker's opinion).
Trivial = unimportant
Unwind = to begin the process of relaxation after stress or hard work
Foster = to protect something and encourage it to grow (an idea, an attitude, a feeling, an action or a result).

Exercise

Choose a word or phrase from the definitions above and write it in the correct gap below.

- If there is more than one possible answer, choose the best option for the sentence.

- You might need to use the same word or phrase more than once in some cases.

- You may need to adapt the form of the word to fit into the sentence. For example, you might need to change a verb to third person singular to ensure subject-verb agreement like *bond-bonds.*

1. I decided to .... myself and had a weekend in New York.

2. I usually like to .... by doing some exercise and meeting up with some friends at the weekend. We have a few drinks and go out for dinner or we watch a film. I also like to unwind at the end of the day by reading and listening to some music. It really helps to clear my mind.

3. Lots of decisions that we think are really important when we're younger seem .... when we get older.

4. I found paragliding .... I was hooked from the first time I tried it.

5. I really want to study and work in London, because it's such a .... place. I love walking down the street and seeing all the different people from all over the world, or, going to the markets and chatting to the locals.

6. The film was ...., I couldn't take my eyes off the screen (it had us glued to the screen). From the plot, to the characters and setting, I thought it was all incredible.

7. I want to .... a career in engineering.

8. I find numbers and Maths quite ...., I'm much more interested in biology.

9. The government has introduced policies that .... fair competition among companies.

10. Turning up to a formal office job interview in shorts is not .... obviously, so they rejected him. This made him re-examine his life.

11. I live quite a .... life during the week. I live in a small apartment in the city centre and I work and study most days. However, at the weekends, I work as a magician at private events around the country!

12. According to .... wisdom in Hollywood, films can't make a profit unless they have big name actors and actresses and large budgets. I really like films that defy those odds.

    *Note: 'defy the odds' means to succeed despite what people believe or despite low probability of success.

13. There is a .... of people who agree with this political party's policies, but the majority of the population are against them.

14. People judge you based on how you .... yourself more than on how you dress, even though the way you dress is also a big factor.

15. There is too much .... on young people today. People expect us to have everything figured out by the time we're 18, but that doesn't usually happen. I know people who are in the 40s and are still figuring their life out and deciding what they want to do!

16. Social media and the internet in general have changed our ....

17. My favourite band, the Snake Patrol, were not very well known when they started, but then they released that song 'Slither in the Wind' and they became .... Suddenly, everyone was listening to them.

18. It's important to .... with your class mates because it makes projects easier and it helps you learn faster, as you can learn from each other.

19. I really admire my father because he refuses to .... to what society dictates. When people told him that he should go to university and study law, he refused. Instead, he started his own business when he had no money and he made it successful through hard work and effort.

20. When you train for an important football match, it's important to keep a positive .... and constantly try to make small improvements. It's important to view your mistakes as lessons rather than failures.

TOPIC 4. EDUCATION

Theoretical = coming from theories, not practice. It's another way of saying that something has not been proven in the real world. Theoretical is also used as an adjective to describe something that focuses on abstract concepts rather than practicing a skill.

Acquire = to buy with money, get by chance or gain through effort.

Please *Note: It's quite a formal verb, so it is often used in every day conversation with a little bit of irony. It's used as a colourful alternative to 'buy', 'get', or 'gain' in informal conversations. In formal conversations, it's often used in interviews (to talk about skills or experience you have acquired) or speaking exams like IELTS.

Valid = acceptable or reasonable

Determine = find out, discover or decide after doing research

Establish = prove or consolidate
Significant = meaningful or important
Miscalculation = a mistake, using bad judgment or making an error in a calculation.
Methodical = being organised or careful and patient when you do something.
Cram = to overload the brain by trying to learn a lot in a short period of time.
Compulsory = obligatory, something you HAVE to do

Exercise

Choose a word or phrase from the definitions above and write it in the correct gap below.

- If there is more than one possible answer, choose the best option for the sentence.

- You might need to use the same word or phrase more than once in some cases.

- You may need to adapt the form of the word to fit into the sentence. For example, you might need to change a verb to third person singular to ensure subject-verb agreement like *bond-bonds*.

1. First, I have to .... whether I should study a Masters' degree or whether I should try to gain more industry experience.

2. Talk about a .... day in your life.
    You should say:
    When it was.
    What happened.
    Why it was .... and how it made you feel.

Answer: *Ok, the most meaningful/important day I can remember is blah blah blah*

3. They should .... where the virus came from first, and then establish ways to prevent this from happening again in the future.

4. I always say that I'm going to be really organised for my tests, but I always end up .... it all in at the last minute!

5. I think that choosing this venue for the event was a .... on my part, as they were completely unprepared and didn-t offer any of the services they advertised. I really should have checked their reviews first.

6. I think that in order to be as successful as possible at university, you need to be .... by always keeping an organised *Notebook and by always categorising your *Notes into sections.

7. I believe that it should be .... to have some sort of practical training as part of your degree. I think

that getting industry experience is vital in today's job market.

> *Note: 'Industry experience' is a term which literally means experience of working in the sector where you want to be employed. (It can be work experience placements or full-time jobs you've had in the past)

8. I recently .... a new watch, which I have completely fallen in love with!

9. The idea that time-travel is possible is purely .... We don't actually know because it is currently impossible to test the theory.

10. You make a .... point. (This means: 'What you're saying is fair').

11. I think it's important to have a .... component in a Business course so you can understand certain concepts, but you also need a practical component, so you can learn how to implement those concepts in the real world.

12. Talk about something you've .... recently.

> *You should mention:*

What It is
When you .... it.
How you .... it and why it's important to you.

*Note: In this example you could talk about something you have bought or a skill you have obtained through your efforts.

TOPIC 5: ADVERTISING

Persuade = convince someone of something
Unavoidable = certain to happen
Effective = when something achieves its purpose
Ploy = trick
Intrusive = invasive
Hype-up = a phrasal verb meaning to exaggerate for a commercial or public relations interest **Hype**= we also use 'hype' as a noun meaning exaggeration (usually for commercial reasons)
Endorse = officially recommend a product or a company
Gullible = too trusting or easy to trick
Prominent = noticeable or extraordinary

Entice = tempt by offering something
Bombard = continuously direct something towards someone
Inescapable = something you can't avoid.

Exercise

Choose a word or phrase from the definitions above and write it in the correct gap below.

- If there is more than one possible answer, choose the best option for the sentence.

- You might need to use the same word or phrase more than once in some cases.

- You may need to adapt the form of the word to fit into the sentence. For example, you might need to change a verb to third person singular to ensure subject-verb agreement like *bond-bonds*.

1. If you allow advertisers to promote gambling, people will gamble more. It's ....

2. We are constantly .... with adverts every day on TV, online, on the radio, in newspapers and even on the street. It seems like everywhere we look there's an advert.

477

3. I think we are all quite .... as consumers. We often believe companies just because they advertise on TV.

4. It seems like everywhere we look there's an advert, it's

....

5. Fast food companies .... us with adverts of delicious looking food, but when you actually try it, it's often disappointing.

6. .... advertising sells products and creates brand awareness.

7. A .... marketing guru argues that all publicity, whether it's positive or negative, is actually good for a company.

8. Shops use special discounts as a marketing .... to encourage people to go into their shops and buy other products. People go into the shop for the discount and end up buying products that are not on discount.

9. I find .... advertising like internet popups and cookies really annoying.

10. The role of advertising is to .... customers to buy products they don't necessarily need.

11. It's important to ignore the .... when you're trying to choose a good restaurant.

12. Most companies .... their products to sell more.

13. Nike are .... by famous professional footballers all over the world.

Topic 6: Travel & places

Memorable = something special or unforgettable
Custom = a local tradition or habit
Remote = isolated or far away
Spectacular = stunning, amazing or very impressive
Landscape = large natural area of land
Basic = simple, not complicated or luxurious. (Often used to describe accommodation)
Barren = without vegetation
Wander = walk without a specific destination

Exercise

Choose a word or phrase from the definitions above and write it in the correct gap below.

- If there is more than one possible answer, choose the best option for the sentence.

- You might need to use the same word or phrase more than once in some cases.

- You may need to adapt the form of the word to fit into the sentence. For example, you might need to change a verb to third person singular to ensure subject-verb agreement like *bond-bonds.*

1. It's a .... to eat cheese and cold-cuts in Mediterranean countries such as Spain and Italy.

2. On our first day in Berlin, we .... around the city and explored different markets and bars around the centre.

3. The landscape is quite ...., but it's stunningly beautiful. The sunsets in particular are amazing.

4. During our trip to Thailand, we visited a .... island just off the coast of Phuket. It was spectacular.

5. When I visited Bangkok, I ate the most .... food and the temples were absolutely stunning.

6. The South of Spain has some amazing .... In some areas, you can go skiing in the mornings and then go to the hot beach in the afternoon. It's stunning.

7. Our hotel was really ...., but we only used it as a place to sleep. We spent most of our time outside, exploring the city and going on guided tours. It was an amazing experience.

8. Traveling round America with my family was a .... experience. We managed to visit six states in total and did an amazing road trip down Route 66.

TOPIC 7: ANIMALS

Endangered = a species of animal or plant that's dying.
Venomous = poisonous
Domesticated = trained to live with humans in houses instead of in the wild.
Thrive = grow strong
Vulnerable = something that can be hurt or that is in danger.
Dwindle = shrink in numbers, become fewer or weaker
Habitat = Natural environment of an animal or plant species.
Survival = continuing to exist
Co-exist = live in the same time or place

Exercise

Choose a word or phrase from the definitions above and write it in the correct gap below.

- If there is more than one possible answer, choose the best option for the sentence.

- You might need to use the same word or phrase more than once in some cases.

- You may need to adapt the form of the word to fit into the sentence. For example, you might need to change a verb to third person singular to ensure subject-verb agreement like *bond-bonds*.

1. We must put stricter systems in place in order to ensure the .... of species such as chimpanzees, mountain gorillas and orangutans.

2. The large human presence in the area has had a negative effect on fish ....

3. Higher penalties could stop smugglers, protect public health and help preserve .... species such as tigers.

4. While many animals are already facing and will continue to face serious problems due to global warming, some species will actually .... on a warming planet.

5. Humans can .... with plants and other animals, we just need to see it as a major priority. I strongly believe that in ten or twenty-years-time it will be too late to reverse the effects of global warming. We must act now; our survival depends on it.

6. The Mountain Gorilla is one of the most critically .... animals on the planet.

7. Scientists recently created the largest botanical dataset ever and discovered that almost 40% of plant species that live on land are potentially .... to global warming. If we don't make radical changes now, we risk losing these species in the next few years. This will be carry disastrous consequences for human beings.

8. I think it's important to remember that not all animals can be or should be .... I honestly believe that people should not be allowed to have pets like snakes, birds or monkeys. It's cruel and potentially dangerous in my opinion.

9. Many people assume that most snakes are poisonous, but of the 3,500 snake species around the world, only 600 are actually ....

TOPIC 8: TECHNOLOGY AND COMPUTERS

Virtual = in a computer or simulation, not in the real world
Digital = computerised rather than physical. Often used to refer to information and information products.
Embrace = happily accept
Addictive = when something makes people want more and more
Security (Secure) = Safety (Safe)
Cutting-edge = the newest or most advanced technology, design or method.
Cyberbullying = attacking other people online
Technological = relate to technology
Dated = not relevant or true anymore because things have changed

Domestic appliances = machines we use in our homes

'White-goods', means domestic appliances like washing machines and dishwashers, but doesn't usually include devices like blenders or air fryers for example.

Surpass = Be or do more than. Do something better than or be better than. Be bigger than, higher than, faster than etc.

Upgrade = get a better-quality version of something

Innovative = creative and new

Exercise

Choose a word or phrase from the definitions above and write it in the correct gap below.

-   If there is more than one possible answer, choose the best option for the sentence.

-   You might need to use the same word or phrase more than once in some cases.

-   You may need to adapt the form of the word to fit into the sentence. For example, you might need to change a verb to third person singular to ensure subject-verb agreement like *bond-bonds*.

1. As humans, we continually strive to .... what we can do and what we think is possible. I think it's mind-boggling to think about the technology we might have in 1-200 years, and the things that will be possible in 500 years. It just blows my mind!

    *Note: 'mind-boggling' means 'amazing' or 'incredible'. 'It blows my mind' or it's 'mind blowing' means the same. It's something so amazing or interesting, that it excites you and makes you feel a sense of wonder.

2. Sales of .... books, or e-books, have been rising steadily for years now.

3. My favourite possession is my new phone. I bought it last week. This particular model contains a .... processor which makes it 50% faster than the previous model from the same brand. I also love the design, as it's sleek and robust at the same time.

   *Note: 'Sleek' means smooth or stylish, while 'robust' means strong and durable. In the example you could have also talked about its '................ design' instead of its processor.

4. .... is a huge issue nowadays, because victims cannot escape the bullying.

5. It would be an absolute game-changer if the government could introduce a policy of upgrading .... technology with cutting-edge energy efficient models, improving performance and energy consumption.

   *Note: a 'game-changer' or 'game-changing', means a radical change (usually positive). Something that would change everything if it was applied in this example.

6. .... form part of a multi-billion-dollar industry. Although many of them are extremely handy, we often end up buying devices we don't need and that don't even make our lives any easier. *Note: 'Handy' means convenient.

7. The .... era has brought many benefits to our lives. In my opinion, it has massively improved human interaction by providing us with more options to connect with people from all over the planet and to keep in touch with family and friends when we're far away. It has allowed us to communicate during times of crisis and it allows us to work together for common goals. None of this was possible (would have been possible) thirty years ago.

8. Some of the most .... inventions in human history have been born out of pure necessity. It's a total cliché, but necessity really is the mother of invention.

   *Note: 'Necessity is the mother of invention' is an expression in English and in several other languages. It means that humans invent things they need. In times of extreme need we think of our most creative ideas in order to survive.

9. I know it's a bit of a cliché, but I still believe that .... reality is the future of entertainment.

10. I think that as a society, we're not paying enough attention to the fact that technology is very .... While it can be extremely beneficial, there are also many potential drawbacks.

    **Note: 'drawbacks' is like saying 'disadvantages'

11. Data .... is a massive issue at the moment, and rightfully so. Companies hold a lot of information about us, and it would be dangerous in the wrong hands.

    *Note: 'and rightfully so', is an informal phrase we use at the end of sentences to state that what we've just mentioned is justified.

    Examples could be:
    Smoking has been banned in public spaces, and rightfully so!

    When they didn't send her the product she'd paid for, she demanded her money back, and rightfully so!

12. Not everyone has .... this new era of reading on your phone or on other electronic devices. Many people still prefer to read books the traditional way.

13. We decided to .... our kitchen, replacing all of our outdated appliances with new cutting-edge ones.

TOPIC 9: FASHION

Shoppers = people who buy from retail stores.
Passing = short. Something that will disappear quickly
Trendy = fashionable
Impulsive = an action carried out without thinking. Or a person who doesn't think before acting.
Consumerism = the behaviour or culture of buying things we don't necessarily need.
Purchase = in the noun form, this means something that has been bought. In the verb form, it means 'buy'.

Exercise

Choose a word or phrase from the definitions above and write it in the correct gap below.

- If there is more than one possible answer, choose the best option for the sentence.

- You might need to use the same word or phrase more than once in some cases.

- You may need to adapt the form of the word to fit into the sentence. For example, you might need to change a verb to third person singular to ensure subject-verb agreement like *bond-bonds.*

1. I believe that some people choose clothes only because they are ...., but I don't think most people do that. I think most people choose the clothes they like within the current trends.

2. The most memorable thing I've ever .... is my car. It gives me independence and freedom, so I can go wherever I want. It allows me to study and work and it allows me to visit my friends and family. Having it has completely changed my life for the better.

3. I really hope responsible fashion isn't a .... trend. I hope that the top brands in the industry will take a more active role in the near-future, as more people recognise the importance of being environmentally-conscious.

4. .... buying is a habit that I would like to stop! Whenever I go to a shopping centre I always end up buying something. I find it really hard to resist!

5. I think .... is mostly negative, because it makes us focus on things that aren't important. Many people put more time and effort into obtaining material possessions than they do into improving themselves as human beings.

6. *Examiner Question:* Why do some people enjoy clothes shopping?

   Candidate Answer: Good question! I think some .... enjoy the experience of walking around the different shops trying things on. Many people also go with friends or family and make it into a social outing. They go for lunch, or for coffee, or they go to the cinema after shopping.

7. I had to borrow money to .... my first car.

TOPIC 10: CITY LIFE

Inadequate = not good enough
Transportation (transport) = the type of vehicle you use to travel
Pedestrian = person walking on the street
Commute = In the noun form, this means your journey to school or work. In the verb for, it means to travel to work or school.
Pavement = the place where pedestrians should walk on the street (not the road).
Slums = very poor-quality housing, often without running water or electricity.
Infrastructure = services and basic structures in an area. Infra- means 'below;' so the infrastructure is the 'basic structure below' a country, an economy, a business or an organisation.
Overpopulated (overpopulation)= when there are too many people in an area.

Outskirts = the edge of a city, town or village.	
Isolated = separated from others	
Inequality = The opposite of equality. Disparity or imbalance in something. Often used to talk about people's rights or living standards.	
Overwhelmed = unable to deal with a situation	
Shortage = a lack of something	
Affluent = rich / wealthy / prosperous	
Run-down = when talking about things it means old and neglected. When talking about humans, 'run-down' means tired-looking or looking slightly ill.	

Exercise

Choose a word or phrase from the definitions above and write it in the correct gap below.

- If there is more than one possible answer, choose the best option for the sentence.

- You might need to use the same word or phrase more than once in some cases.

- You may need to adapt the form of the word to fit into the sentence. For example, you might need to change a verb to third person singular to ensure subject-verb agreement like *bond-bonds.*

1. I found Amsterdam to be very ....-friendly, as there are very few cars, and the bikes there are quite respectful of the people walking around.

2. Water .... cause major problems in some areas of the country.

3. Public .... in my home town is great. There are buses every fifteen minutes and train lines every twenty

minutes. You can be anywhere in town within twenty minutes.

4. One third of the people in the city live in .... They don't have electricity or running water.

5. More funding is required to boost the crumbling ....of the country's production plants.

   *Notes:
   Funding = Money
   Required = Needed
   Boost = Improve or revitalise
   Crumbling = decaying or run-down

6. I have to .... for one hour every day to get to class!

7. The .... are quite run-down in my neighbourhood, but the council don't have enough money to fix them.

8. Half of the city's population live in .... housing. The conditions are quite bad for these people, as most of them don't have running water.

9. I grew up on the .... of the city, but I moved closer to the centre when I started working. The commute was just too long to do every day!

10. The .... in urban areas has led to an increase in pollution and inadequate housing among other issues. This is something that needs to be addressed sooner rather than later.

   *Note: 'sooner rather than later' is an expression to emphasise that something needs to be done now not in the future.

11. John Milton proposed a new system designed to remove .... in health care but it was rejected by his own political party.

12. The healthcare system was initially ....by the sheer number of infections. They couldn't handle it.

   *Note: the word 'sheer' is used to express that the only thing that affected the situation was the thing you're talking about. In the example, 'the number of infections', the number of infections was the only or main cause of the problem.

13. When I travelled round Mexico, I visited an ....
community in the middle of the desert. It was really
interesting. Most of the people there had never seen a
foreigner before, so they were really curious. They were
so welcoming and kind that I actually felt a bit sad when I
had to leave.

14. Some parts of my city are quite ...., but the
centre is very nice to walk around and has many hidden
gems.

15. I really admire my uncle Bob, because he grew up in a
very deprived area, but he managed to set up several
businesses and he now lives in one of the most
.... areas in town. I admire his drive and
ambition, as well as his creativity.

*Notes:
Deprived= poor
Grow up= when you're raised in a certain place
Set up = start businesses or projects
Drive= Determination (refusing to be defeated)

TOPIC 11: ENVIRONMENT

Agricultural= connected to raising animals for food and growing fruits and vegetables by cultivating the soil and producing crops.
Renewable = something that can be produced again and again
Logging = systematically cutting down trees
Vital = essential for the existence of something
Irrigation = systems to supply areas with water.
Pressing = urgent
Pollutant = a substance that contaminates
Ecosystem = the environment in an area and all the biological life in it

Unprecedented = something that has never happened before
Safeguard = protect against something

Exercise

Choose a word or phrase from the definitions above and write it in the correct gap below.

- If there is more than one possible answer, choose the best option for the sentence.

- You might need to use the same word or phrase more than once in some cases.

- You may need to adapt the form of the word to fit into the sentence. For example, you might need to change a verb to third person singular to ensure subject-verb agreement like *bond-bonds.*

1. Trees are .... for the environment.

2. We must .... the environment against the destruction of habitats and the over-exploitation of natural resources such as fresh water and fisheries among other issues.

3. The most dangerous gaseous air .... released into the air in urban areas are Sulphur dioxide, nitrogen dioxide, and carbon monoxide;

505

4. I grew up in an .... community so farming was still in my blood.

5. .... is a major issue in many forests and jungles all over the world. As more trees are chopped down, these natural areas are shrinking more and more.

6. Trees are .... natural resources, but they should be treated with extreme care.

7. Lack of investment in new methods may result in deterioration of the .... system in the area and a subsequent decline of the local economy.

   *Notes:

   Deterioration= decay. When something breaks down and dissolves

   Subsequent= eventual. When something happens as a result of something else.

8. There is a .... need for housing in the area.

9. Half of these trees could be gone within five years,
   threatening jobs and ....

10. Governments were not sure how to deal with the
    situation because it was .... in 21st-century life.

TOPIC 12: MEDIA

Tabloid = newspapers that are not as serious and impartial
Impartial = neutral
Biased = not neutral or impartial
Escapism = a noun to describe when you use something to forget about normal life and escape your problems.
Medium = singular noun for media. Media is plural (most people don't realise).
Well informed = having enough high-quality information to understand and make good decisions
Scrutinise = examine or analyse carefully
Censor = to remove parts of what is said or published in the media or in any form of communication because you don't want someone to see, read or hear that information.

Manipulate = to control someone or something indirectly (has a negative connotation)

Spotlight = public attention / publicity / limelight / being in the public eye

Imply = to suggest something without saying it directly

Exercise

Choose a word or phrase from the definitions above and write it in the correct gap below.

- If there is more than one possible answer, choose the best option for the sentence.

- You might need to use the same word or phrase more than once in some cases.

- You may need to adapt the form of the word to fit into the sentence. For example, you might need to change a verb to third person singular to ensure subject-verb agreement like *bond-bonds.*

1. The President's blunders gave the .... press great satisfaction.

2. The media .... that there had been a cover-up. They never said it directly, but it was the logical conclusion from the way they reported the whole story.

   *Note: a 'cover-up' is when governments or businesses try to stop the public from finding out about something serious.

3. It's important to .... politicians to ensure that they are honest and trustworthy.

4. Interactive series and films open up the .... of video platforms to the participation of viewers.

5. For many people watching fantasy series and films on Netflix or on TV is a form of ....

6. I think the government and the media .... us in many ways. They report the news the way they want us to see it.

7. The tabloid press gave a very .... account of the situation.

   *Note: the word 'account' means 'report' in this context.

8. I completely disagree with any initiatives which aim to .... the Internet in any way, shape or form.

   *Note: 'in any way, shape or form' means 'in any way', but adds extra emphasis.

9. A judge has to be fair and ...., or the law loses all meaning.

   *Note: when something 'loses all meaning', we mean that it loses its purpose or value in some way.

10. Consumers need to be .... about the side effects of so-called natural remedies.

   *Note: 'So-called' is used to communicate to the listener that you believe a word that is used to describe someone or something is wrong in some way.

11. I think many celebrities struggle with living their lives in the .... It must be very hard to have every part of your life scrutinised by strangers.

FULL NOTES SECTION WITH ANSWERS

TOPIC 1. PEOPLE

Acquaintance= (n) when you know someone well enough to say hello and talk to them when you see them, but they're not a friend. For example: I don't know her very well, she's not really a friend, she's more of an acquaintance.
Sibling = brother or sister For example: The shop offers a discount for siblings who sign up for store cards.
Characteristic = typical For example: Adding soy sauce while you're cooking the vegetables gives the dish its characteristic Vietnamese flavour.
Resemble = when something looks similar to something else, it resembles that thing. For example: Porche's new 2020 car model resembles the old 1970s models.
Reliable = something or someone that can be trusted for functional things (something or someone you can rely on). For example: It's important for me that my friends are reliable, I don't

like people who are late or who cancel plans at the last minute.

My car is very reliable, it has never broken down.

*Note: the opposite is 'unreliable'

Bond = means a close link or to form a close link if we use it as a verb

For example (noun): I'm very close to my family, we have a very strong bond.

For example (verb): It's important for people to bond if they work together closely. It's easier to do this in small offices rather than big offices. This is why I prefer working for small companies, as they tend to have a smaller, friendlier environment.

Conscious = when your conscious of something it means you're aware of something.

For example: I'm conscious that I will need to work very hard to become a doctor, but it's my dream and I'm wiling to make the sacrifice.

Inherent = a natural part of something is inherent to that thing.

For example: Getting into a car accident is one of the inherent dangers of driving, so it's very important that drivers pay full attention on the road so we can minimise the risk.

Self-esteem = the level confidence or belief you have in your own abilities and positive qualities. For example: Studies suggest that people with higher self-esteem are more likely to be successful in their careers. *Note: Self-esteem is often described as 'high' or 'low'.
Stereotypical = something that fits into the typical ideas about the way it should be. For example: I want to study accounting, but I don't think I'm the stereotypical accountant. The stereotypical accountant is a very organised and methodical person who enjoys siting at a desk crunching numbers (making calculations).
Tendency = something that happens repeatedly. Trend. For example: There is a tendency nowadays to socialise through technology. I think it has some very clear benefits, but it needs to be used in moderation. The benefits are X, Y and Z. However, the dangers are A, B and C.
Gender = the sex of a person. For example: In my opinion, gender is sadly still and issue we need to tackle in today's workplace. There are still great disparities between male and female employees in terms of wages and opportunities.
Lifetime = the period of time that something exists or that

a person or an animal lives.

For example: Certain types of bird only live in one place in their entire lifetime.

Sympathise = when you sympathise with someone it means that you understand their position and situation. It's similar to having empathy.

For example: I really sympathise with all the people who lost their jobs, because nobody wants to be in that situation. I think the government can do more to help them at the moment by doing X, Y and Z for example.

Hardwired = instinctive behaviour

For example: I think our desire to improve and grow is hardwired into us as humans, but it needs to be stimulated. This is why I strongly believe that we need to promote real-world, practical education. If people see that they can learn real-world skills, it will encourage them to keep learning.

Habitually = usually

For example: White sharks do not habitually attack humans, unless they confuse them with seals. However, they have a really bad reputation, and I think this has contributed to a lot of shark deaths over the years, as they've been actively hunted in many parts of the world.

Topic 2. Health & Medicine

Allergic = when you have a negative physical reaction to a substance.

For example: I'm allergic to nuts, so I need to be very careful when I eat out in restaurants.

Harmful = not safe, bad for a person or bad for something.

For example: Smoking is very harmful not just to the person smoking, but also to the people around. This is why we need to make it illegal in my opinion.

For example: The pandemic has been very harmful to businesses all over the world.

Appetite/hunger = your desire for something (usually food).

For example: I think junk food increases your appetite, as it has very little substance. It doesn't fill you for long and makes you crave more.

*Note: 'crave' means when you really want something. A strong desire for something.

Lifestyle = the way someone lives their life. Your lifestyle can be active, sedentary, sociable, etc...

For example: I don't think I could ever work in an office, as I don't think I'd like that lifestyle. I'm an active person who enjoys doing things outdoors and moving around a lot, and staying in one place indoors for 8-12 hours a day everyday is my idea of hell!

Ingredients = the components of a specific medicine, drink, food or dish.

For example: I believe that the government needs to introduce tighter restrictions to regulate the ingredients of natural remedies, as they are often potentially dangerous.

For example: My favourite dish is peperoni pizza. The ingredients are pizza dough, cheese, tomato, peperoni, olive oil and chilly.

Nutritious = full of vitamins, fat, protein, carbohydrates or other essential components for good health.

For example: Avocados are very nutritious, they are packed with iron, vitamins and healthy fat.

Suffer = feel discomfort or pain. It can also be used to describe when something negative happens to you or when you have a negative health condition.

For example: I suffered quite a lot during the lockdown, as I couldn't visit my family.

For example: Jack suffered a car accident when he was younger, and it changed his life. He is now extremely successful and responsible.

For example: People who suffer from rare genetic disorders need more guidance from doctors.

Sedentary = the opposite of active. This is often used to describe jobs, activities and lifestyle.

For example: I need to exercise more because I have a very sedentary job, where I spend most of the day sitting down at a desk.

Psychological = related to psychology or the mind.

For example: The psychological impact of what has happened has been enormous. It has changed the way we live and the way we view the world.

Beneficial = good, positive or helpful.

For example: It would be beneficial if we could have more telecommuting from now on, as it reduces potential risks and reduces damage to the environment. It is also cheaper for many companies, so everyone would benefit from this type of change.

Detrimental = bad or negative. Not helpful

For example: Too much sugar can be extremely detrimental to your health.

Intake = the amount you eat or drink.

For example: It's important to monitor your daily intake of trans fats.

Eradicate = get rid or something (exterminate)

For example: We need to eradicate the problem now or it will cause more damage in the future.

Well-being = your well-being is your level of comfort, health and happiness. For example: Our well-being is more important than money. We need to focus on this so that we can eradicate this problem.
Severity = the seriousness of something. For example: We underestimated the severity of the situation.
Preventive = actions that aim to prevent or stop something For example: Preventive medicine is often more effective than treatment. For example: The government has put preventive measures in place so that businesses can recover as quickly as possible.
Additives = the chemicals that are added to food and drink to stop it from rotting or to enhance favour. Preservatives = the chemicals that are added to food and drink to keep it fresh for longer. For example: It's better for your health of you avoid eating too many foods that contain additives / preservatives.
Administer= to give a patient a medicine or medical treatment.

For example: The drug is administered orally, twice a day.

Admit = to officially allow someone to stay in hospital for medical care.

For example: The more people are admitted into hospitals, the higher the demand on medical staff and other resources.

Agony = intense physical pain or emotional suffering.

For example: When I broke my leg I was in agony, so I rang my friend and she took me to hospital.

For example: It was agonising/agony when my team lost the championship in the last 3 seconds of the game! (This is an exaggeration)

For example: Having your heart broken is agony/agonising.

Antidote = a drug that stops the negative effects of a poison.

For example: If you get bitten by a poisonous snake, it's important to go to hospital so they can give you an antidote.

Consultant = an experienced doctor in a hospital who specialises in a specific area of medicine.

For example: He works as a cardiology consultant at a children's hospital in the city centre. His work is very demanding but he's passionate about it.

Diagnosis = an official conclusion about a patient's condition, given by a doctor.

For example: My uncle was diagnosed with Crohn's disease several years ago, but he still works full-time and hasn't let it stop him from pursuing most of his hobbies.

Inoculate = to use a vaccine protect people against a disease (to vaccinate)

For example: A funny story happened to me on my last birthday. I took my dog to get inoculated against rabies and someone had brought an abandoned dog into the vet's to try and help it. Long story short, I ended up adopting another dog!

Nursing home (Care home) = a place where the elderly live when they are not able to look after themselves due to their age or due to an illness.

For example: There has been a lot of controversy surrounding the level of care in some nursing homes.

TOPIC 3. SOCIAL & LEISURE

Conform = to follow social rules.

For example: I really admire my father because he refuses to conform to what society dictates. When people told him that he should go to university and study law, he refused. Instead, he started his own business when he had no money and he made it successful through hard work and effort.

Cooperate = when people work well together

For example: It's important to cooperate with your class mates because it makes projects easier and it helps you learn faster, as you can learn from each other.

Mindset (frame of mind) = the way you think. Your mental attitude at a particular point in your life or in a particular situation.

For example: When you train for an important football match, it's important to keep a positive mindset and constantly try to make small improvements. It's important to view your mistakes as lessons rather than failures.

Minority = a small percentage of a group or population.

For example: There is a minority of people who agree with this political party's policies, but the majority of the population are against them.

Shun = to reject

For example: We can't shun our responsibility as citizens. We have to be sensible and responsible to prevent dangerous situations like this from happening again.

Conventional = the usual, normal or traditional way of doing something or thinking. 'Conventional wisdom' is an expression, meaning: what most people believe to be true, or what most experts accept as the truth.

For example: I live quite a conventional life during the week. I live in a small apartment in the city centre and I work and study most days. However, at the weekends, I work as a magician at private events around the country! I love it because...........

For example: According to conventional wisdom in Hollywood, films can't make a profit unless they have big name actors and actresses and large budgets. I really like films that defy those odds, such as ...

*Note: 'defy the odds' means to succeed despite what people believe or despite low probability of success.

Interaction = communication between people (written, spoken or through sign language for example).

For example: Social media and the internet in general have changed our interactions (the way we interact).

Pressure = stress or expectations.

For example: There is too much pressure on young people today. People expect us to have everything figured out by the time we're 18, but that doesn't usually happen. I know people who are in the 40s and are still figuring their life out and deciding what they want to do!

Conduct = This can be used as verb and as a noun meaning behaviour-behave

For example: People judge you based on how you conduct yourself more than on how you dress, even though the way you dress is also a big factor.

Mainstream = common likes or ideas.

For example: My favourite band, the Snake Patrol, were not very well known when they started, but then they released that song 'Slither in the Wind' and they became mainstream. Everyone was listening to them.

Appropriate = acceptable or suitable for a particular situation.

For example: Turning up to a formal office job interview in shorts is not appropriate obviously, so they rejected him. This made him re-examine his life.

Foster = to protect something and encourage it to grow (an idea, an attitude, a feeling, an action or a result).

For example: The government has introduced policies that foster fair competition among companies.

Multicultural = something that has several different cultures. It can be a team, a department, a city, a country etc..

For example: I really want to study and work in London, because it's such a multicultural place. I love walking down the street and seeing all the different people from all over the world, or going to the markets and chatting to the locals.

Absorbing = something that entertains you so much, that you forget about everything else.

For example: The film was absorbing, I couldn't take my eyes off the screen (it had us glued to the screen). From the plot, to the characters and setting, I thought it was all incredible.

Exhilarating = something that makes you feel full of energy and excitement. Thrilling.

For example: I found paragliding exhilarating. I was hooked from the first time I tried it.

Indulge = to do something that you like (like a reward).

For example: I decided to indulge myself and had a weekend in New York.

Pursue = to follow an activity in order to reach a goal. Think of chasing your dreams.

For example: I want to pursue a career in engineering.

Tedious = not exciting. Focusing on highly specific but boring things (in the speaker's opinion).

For example: I find numbers and Maths quite tedious, I'm much more interested in biology.

Trivial = unimportant

For example: Lots of decisions that we think are really important when we're younger seem trivial when we get older.

Unwind = to begin the process of relaxation after stress or hard work

For example: I usually like to unwind by doing some exercise and meeting up with some friends at the weekend. We have a few drinks and go out for dinner or we watch a film. I also like to unwind at the end of the day by reading and listening to some music. It really helps to clear my mind.

TOPIC 4. EDUCATION

Theoretical = coming from theories, not practice. It's another way of saying that something has not been proven in the real world. Theoretical is also used as an adjective to describe something that focuses on abstract concepts rather than practicing a skill.

For example: The idea that time-travel is possible is purely theoretical. We don't actually know because it is currently impossible to test the theory.

For example: I think it's important to have a theoretical component in a Business course so you can understand certain concepts, but you also need a practical component so you can learn how to implement those concepts in the real world.

Acquire = to buy with money, get by chance or gain through effort.

For example: I recently acquired a new watch, which I have completely fallen in love with!

Please *Note: It's quite a formal verb, so it is often used in every day conversation with a little bit of irony. It's used as a colourful alternative to 'buy', 'get', or 'gain' in informal conversations.

In formal conversations, it's often used in interviews or speaking exams such as the IELTS test.

For example: Talk about something you've acquired recently.

You should mention:

What It is
When you acquired it.
How you acquired it
Why it's important to you.

Compulsory = obligatory, something you HAVE to do

For example: I believe that it should be compulsory to have some sort of practical training as part of your degree. I think that getting industry experience is vital in today's job market.

*Note: 'Industry experience' is a term which literally means experience of working in the sector where you want to be employed. (It can be work experience placements or full-time jobs you've had in the past)

Valid = acceptable or reasonable

For example: You make a valid point. (This means: 'What you're saying is fair').

Determine = find out or discover

For example: First, I have to determine whether I should study a Master's degree or whether I should try to gain more industry experience.

Establish = prove or consolidate

531

For example: They should establish where the virus came from first, and then establish ways to prevent this from happening again in the future.

Significant = meaningful or important

For example:

Talk about a significant day in your life.

You should say:

When it was.
What happened.
Why it was significant and how it made you feel.

Answer: Ok, the most meaningful/important day I can remember is ....

Miscalculation = a mistake, using bad judgment or making an error in a calculation.

For example: I think that choosing this venue for the event was a miscalculation on my part, as they were completely unprepared and didn-t offer any of the services they advertised. I really should have checked their reviews first.

Methodical = being organised or careful and patient when you do something.

For example: I think that in order to be as successful as possible at university, you need to be methodical by always keeping an organised *Notebook and by always categorising your *Notes into sections.

Cram = to overload the brain by trying to learn a lot in a short period of time.

For example: I always say that I'm going to be really organised for my tests, but I always end up cramming it all in at the last minute!

TOPIC 5: ADVERTISING

Persuade = convince someone of something For example: The role of advertising is to persuade customers to buy products they don't necessarily need.
Unavoidable = certain For example: If you allow advertisers to promote gambling, people will gamble more. It's unavoidable.
Effective = when something achieves its purpose For example: effective advertising sells products and creates brand awareness.
Ploy = trick For example: Shops use special discounts as a marketing ploy to encourage people to go into their shops and buy other products. People go into the shop for the discount and end up buying products that are not on discount.
Intrusive = invasive For example: I find intrusive advertising like internet popups and cookies really annoying.
Hype-up = exaggerate for a commercial or public relations interest

*Note: we also use 'hype' as a noun meaning exaggeration (usually for commercial reasons)

For example: It's important to ignore the hype when you're trying to choose a good restaurant.

Endorse = officially recommend a product or a company

For example: Nike are endorsed by famous professional footballers all over the world.

Gullible = too trusting or easy to trick

For example: I think we are all quite gullible as consumers. We often believe companies just because they advertise on TV.

Prominent = noticeable or extraordinary

For example: A prominent marketing guru argues that all publicity, whether it's positive or negative, is actually good for a company.

Entice = tempt by offering something

For example: Fast food companies entice us with adverts of delicious looking food, but when you actually try it, it's often disappointing.

Bombard = continuously direct something towards someone

For example: We are constantly bombarded with adverts every day on TV, online, on the radio, in newspapers and even on the street. It seems like everywhere we look there's an advert.

Inescapable = something you can't avoid.

For example: It seems like everywhere we look there's an advert, it's inescapable.

TOPIC 6: TRAVEL & PLACES

Memorable = something special or unforgettable

For example: Traveling round America with my family was a memorable experience. We managed to visit six states in total and did an amazing road trip down Route 66.

Custom = a local tradition or habit

For example: It's a custom to eat cheese and cold-cuts in Mediterranean countries such as Spain and Italy.

Remote = isolated or far away

For example: During our trip to Thailand, we visited a remote island just off the coast of Phuket. It was spectacular.

Spectacular = stunning, amazing or very impressive

For example: When I visited Bangkok, I ate the most spectacular food and the temples were absolutely stunning.

Landscape = large natural area of land

For example: The South of Spain has some amazing landscapes. In some areas, you can go skiing in the mornings and then go to the hot beach in the afternoon. It's stunning.

Basic = simple, not complicated or luxurious. (Often used to describe accommodation)

For example: Our hotel was really basic, but we only used it as a place to sleep. We spent most of our time outside, exploring the city and going on guided tours. It was an amazing experience.

Barren = without vegetation

For example: The landscape is quite barren, but it's stunningly beautiful. The sunsets in particular are amazing.

Wander = walk without a specific destination

For example: On our first day in Berlin, we wandered round the city and explored different markets and bars around the centre.

TOPIC 7: ANIMALS

Endangered = a species of animal or plant that's dying.

For example: The Mountain Gorilla is one of the most critically endangered animals on the planet.

Venomous = poisonous

For example: Many people assume that most snakes are poisonous, but of the 3,500 snake species around the world, only 600 are actually venomous.

Domesticated = trained to live with humans in houses instead of in the wild.

For example: I think it's important to remember that not all animals can be or should be domesticated. I honestly believe that people should not be allowed to have pets like snakes, birds or monkeys. It's cruel and potentially dangerous in my opinion.

Thrive = grow strong

For example: While many animals are already facing and will continue to face serious problems due to global warming, some species will actually thrive on a warming planet.

Vulnerable = something that can be hurt or that is in danger.

For example: Scientists recently created the largest botanical dataset ever, and discovered that almost 40% of plant species that live on land are potentially vulnerable to global warming. If we don't make radical changes now, we risk losing these species in the next few years. This will be carry disastrous consequences for human beings.

Dwindle = shrink in numbers, become fewer or weaker

For example: Higher penalties could stop smugglers, protect public health and help preserve dwindling species such as tigers.

Habitat = Natural environment of an animal or plant species.

For example: The large human presence in the area has had an negative effect on fish habitats.

Survival = continuing to exist

For example: We must put stricter systems in place in order to ensure the survival of species such as chimpanzees, mountain gorillas and orangutans.

Co-exist = live in the same time or place
For example: Humans can co-exist with plants and other animals, we just need to see it as a major priority. I strongly believe that in ten or twenty-years-time it will be too late to reverse the effects of global warming. We must act now; our survival depends on it.

TOPIC 8: TECHNOLOGY AND COMPUTERS

Virtual = in a computer or simulation, not in the real world

For example: I know it's a bit of a cliché, but I still believe that virtual reality is the future of entertainment.

Digital = computerised rather than physical. Often used to refer to information and information products.

For example: Sales of digital books, or e-books, have been rising steadily for years now.

Embrace = happily accept

For example: However, not everyone has embraced this new era of reading on your phone or on other electronic devices. Many people still prefer to read books the traditional way.

Addictive = when something makes people want more and more

For example: I think that as a society, we're not paying enough attention to the fact that technology is very addictive. While it can be extremely beneficial, there are also many potential drawbacks.

*Note: 'drawbacks' is like saying 'disadvantages'

Security (Secure) = Safety (Safe)

For example: Data security is a massive issue at the moment, and rightfully so. Companies hold a lot of information about us, and it would be dangerous in the wrong hands.

*Note: 'and rightfully so', is an informal expression we use at the end of sentences to state that what we've just mentioned is justified.

Examples could be: Smoking has been banned in public spaces, and rightfully so!

When they didn't send her the product she'd paid for, she demanded her money back, and rightfully so!

Cutting-edge = the newest or most advanced technology, design or method.

For example: My favourite possession is my new phone. I bought it last week. This particular model contains a cutting-edge processor which makes it 50% faster than the previous model from the same brand. I also love the design, as it's sleek and robust at the same time.

*Note: 'Sleek' means smooth or stylish, while 'robust' means strong and durable. In the example you could have also talked about its 'cutting-edge design' instead of its processor.

Cyberbullying = attacking other people online

For example: Cyberbullying is a huge issue nowadays, because victims cannot escape the bullying.

Technological = relate to technology

For example: The technological era has brought many benefits to our lives. In my opinion, it has massively improved human interaction by providing us with more options to connect with people from all over the planet and to keep in touch with family and friends when we're far away.

It has allowed us to communicate during times of crisis and it allows us to work together for common goals. None of this was possible (would have been possible) thirty years ago.

Dated = not relevant or true anymore because things have changed

For example: It would be an absolute game-changer if the government could introduce a policy of upgrading dated technology with cutting-edge energy efficient models, improving performance and energy consumption.

*Note: a 'game-changer' or 'game-changing', means a radical change (usually positive). Something that would change everything if it was applied.

Domestic appliances = machines we use in our homes

Domestic appliances are a multi-billion-dollar industry. Although many of them are extremely handy, we often end up buying devices we don't need and that don't even make our lives any easier.

*Notes: 'Handy' means convenient.
'White goods', means domestic appliances like washing machines and dishwashers, but doesn't usually include devices like blenders or air fryers for example.

Surpass = Be or do more than. Do something better than or be better than. Be bigger than, higher than, faster than etc.

For example: As humans, we continually strive to surpass what we can do and what we think is possible. I think it's mind-boggling to think about the technology we might have in 1-200 years, and the things that will be possible in 500 years. It just blows my mind!

*Note: 'mind-boggling' means 'amazing' or 'incredible'.
'It blows my mind' or it's 'mind blowing' means the same. It's something so amazing or interesting, that it excites you and makes you feel a sense of wonder.

Upgrade = get a better-quality version of something

For example: We decided to upgrade our kitchen, replacing all of our outdated appliances with new cutting-edge ones.

Innovative = creative and new

For example: I believe that some of the most innovative inventions in human history have been born out of pure necessity. It's a total cliché, but necessity really is the mother of invention.

*Note: 'Necessity is the mother of invention' is a cliché expression in English and in several other languages. It means that humans invent things they need. In times of extreme need we think of our most creative ideas in order to survive.

TOPIC 9: FASHION

Shoppers = people who buy from retail stores.

For example: Why do some people enjoy clothes shopping?

Good question! I think some shoppers enjoy the experience of walking around the different shops trying things on. Many people also go with friends or family and make it into a social outing. They go for lunch, or for coffee, or they go to the cinema after shopping.

Passing = short. Something that will disappear quickly

For example: I really hope responsible fashion isn't a passing trend. I hope that the top brands in the industry will take a more active role in the near-future, as more people recognise the importance of being environmentally-conscious.

Trendy = fashionable

For example: I believe that some people choose clothes only because they are trendy, but I don't think most people do that. I think most people choose the clothes they like within the current trends.

Impulsive = an action carried out without thinking. Or a person who doesn't think before acting.

For example: Impulsive buying is a habit that I would like to stop! Whenever I go to a shopping centre I always end up buying something. I find it really hard to resist!

Consumerism = the behaviour or culture of buying things we don't necessarily need.

For example: I think consumerism is mostly negative, because it makes us focus on things that aren't important. Many people put more time and effort into obtaining material possessions than they do into improving themselves as human beings.

Purchase = in the noun form, this means something that has been bought. In the verb form, it means 'buy'.

For example: The most memorable thing I've ever purchased is my car. It gives me independence and freedom so I can go wherever I want. It allows me to study and work and it allows me to visit my friends and family. Having it has completely changed my life for the better.

For example (verb): I had to borrow money to purchase my first car.

TOPIC 10: CITY LIFE

Inadequate = not good enough

For example: Half of the city's population live in inadequate housing. The conditions are quite bad for these people, as most of them don't have running water.

Transportation (transport) = the type of vehicle you use to travel

For example: Public transport in my home town is great. There are buses every fifteen minutes and train lines every twenty minutes. You can be anywhere in town within twenty minutes.

Pedestrian = person walking on the street

For example: I found Amsterdam to be very pedestrian-friendly, as there are very few cars, and the bikes there are quite respectful of the people walking around.

Commute = In the noun form, this means your journey to school or work. In the verb for, it means to travel to work or school.

For example: I have to commute for one hour every day to get to class!

Pavement = the place where pedestrians should walk on the street (not the road).

For example: The pavements are quite run-down in my neighbourhood, but the council don't have enough money to fix them.

Slums = very poor-quality housing, often without running water or electricity.

For example: One third of the people in the city live in slums. They don't have electricity or running water.

Infrastructure = services and basic structures in an area. Infra- means 'below;' so the infrastructure is the 'basic structure below' a country, an economy, a business or an organisation.

For example: More funding is required to boost the crumbling infrastructure of the country's production plants.

*Notes:
Funding = Money
Required = Needed
Boost = Improve or revitalise
Crumbling = decaying or run-down

Overpopulated (overpopulation)= when there are too many people in an area.

For example: The overpopulation in urban areas has led to an increase in pollution and inadequate housing among other issues. This is something that needs to be addressed sooner rather than later.

*Note: 'sooner rather than later' is an expression to emphasise that something needs to be done now not in the future.

549

Outskirts = the edge of a city, town or village.

For example: I grew up on the outskirts of the city, but I moved closer to the centre when I started working. The commute was just too long to do every day!

Isolated = separated from others

For example: When I travelled round Mexico, I visited an isolated community in the middle of the desert. It was really interesting. Most of the people there had never seen a foreigner before, so they were really curious. They were so welcoming and kind that I actually felt a bit sad when I had to leave.

Inequality = The opposite of equality. Disparity or imbalance in something. Often used to talk about people's rights or living standards.

For example: John Milton proposed a new system designed to remove inequalities in health care but it was rejected by his own political party.

Overwhelmed = unable to deal with a situation

For example: The healthcare system was initially overwhelmed by the sheer number of infections.

*Note: the word 'sheer' is used to express that the only thing that affected the situation was the thing you're talking about. In the example, 'the number of infections', the number of infections was the only or main cause of the problem.

Shortage = a lack of something

For example: Water shortages cause major problems in some areas of the country.

Affluent = rich / wealthy / prosperous

For example: I really admire my uncle Bob, because he grew up in a very deprived area, but he managed to set up several businesses and he now lives in one of the most affluent areas in town. I admire his drive and ambition, as well as his creativity.

*Notes:
Deprived= poor
Grow up= when you're raised in a certain place
Set up = start businesses or projects
Drive= Determination (refusing to be defeated)

Run-down = when talking about things it means old and neglected.

For example: Some parts of my city are quite run-down, but the centre is very nice to walk around and has........

*Note: When talking about humans, 'run-down' means tired-looking or looking slightly ill.

TOPIC 11: ENVIRONMENT

Agricultural= connected to raising animals for food and growing fruits and vegetables by cultivating the soil and producing crops.

For example: I grew up in an agricultural community so farming was still in my blood.

Renewable = something that can be produced again and again

For example: Trees are renewable natural resources, but they should be treated with extreme care.

Logging = cutting down trees

For example: Logging is a major issue in many forests and jungles all over the world. As more trees are chopped down, these natural areas are shrinking more and more.

Vital = essential for the existence of something

For example: Trees are vital for the environment.

Irrigation = systems to supply areas with water.

For example: Lack of investment in new methods may result in deterioration of the irrigation system in the area and a subsequent decline of the local economy.

*Notes:

Deterioration= decay. When something breaks down and dissolves

Subsequent= eventual. When something happens as a result of something else.

Pressing = urgent

For example: There is a pressing need for housing in the area.

Pollutant = a substance that contaminates

For example: The most dangerous gaseous air pollutants released into the air in urban areas are Sulphur dioxide, nitrogen dioxide, and carbon monoxide;

Ecosystem = the environment in an area and all the biological life in it

For example: Half of these trees could be gone within five years, threatening jobs and ecosystems.

Unprecedented = something that has never happened before

For example: Governments were not sure how to deal with the situation because it was unprecedented in 21st-century life.

Safeguard = protect against something

For example: We must safeguard the environment against the destruction of habitats and the over-exploitation of natural resources such as fresh water and fisheries among other issues.

Topic 12: Media

Tabloid = newspapers that are not as serious and impartial

For example: The President's blunders gave the tabloid press great satisfaction.

Impartial = neutral

For example: A judge has to be fair and impartial, or the law loses all meaning.

*Note: when something 'loses all meaning', we mean that it loses its purpose or value in some way.

Biased = not neutral or impartial

For example: The tabloid press gave a very biased account of the situation.

*Note: the word 'account' means 'report' in this context.

Escapism = a noun to describe when you use something to forget about normal life and escape your problems.

For example: For many people watching fantasy series and films on Netflix or on TV is a form of escapism.

Medium = singular noun for media. Media is plural (most people don't realise).

For example: Interactive series and films open up the medium of video platforms to the participation of viewers.

Well informed = having enough high-quality information to understand and make good decisions

For example: Consumers need to be well informed about the side effects of so-called natural remedies.

*Note: 'So-called' is used to communicate to the listener that you believe a word that is used to describe someone or something is wrong in some way.

Scrutinise = examine or analyse carefully

For example: It's important to scrutinise politicians to ensure that they are honest and trustworthy.

Censor = to remove parts of what is said or published in the media or in any form of communication because you don't want someone to see, read or hear that information.

For example: I completely disagree with any initiatives which aim to censor the Internet in any way, shape or form.

*Note: 'in any way, shape or form' means 'in any way', but adds extra emphasis.

Manipulate = to control someone or something indirectly (has a negative connotation)

For example: I think the government and the media manipulate us in many ways. They report the news the way they want us to see it.

Spotlight = public attention / publicity / limelight / being in the public eye

For example: I think many celebrities struggle with living their lives in the spotlight. It must be very hard to have every part of your life scrutinised by strangers.

Imply = to suggest something without saying it directly

For example: The media implied that there had been a cover-up. They never said it directly, but it was the logical conclusion from the way they reported the whole story.

*Note: a 'cover-up' is when governments or businesses try to stop the public from finding out about something serious.

IELTS LISTENING &
READING
VOCABULARY
DICTIONARY

-A-

Abate: MEANING: Reduce, diminish

SENTENCE: Her stress over spending so much money on her house abated when the real estate broker told her about the property's current market value.

Aberrant: MEANING: Abnormal, deviant

SENTENCE: Running naked down the street might be considered aberrant behaviour.

Abeyance: MEANING: Temporary cessation or suspension

SENTENCE: Her thoughts of her lover were in abeyance while she studied for her exam.

Abridge: MEANING: Condense or shorten

SENTENCE: Audio books are almost always abridged, since few people want to listen to a 200-hour story.

Abscond: MEANING: Leave secretly and hurriedly, often to escape or avoid arrest

SENTENCE: The tenants absconded owing six months' rent.

Abstemious: MEANING: Consuming moderately in something, especially food and drink

SENTENCE: 'We only had one course at dinner.' 'Very abstemious of you.'

Abstruse: MEANING: Difficult to understand

SENTENCE: The doctor's handwriting was so abstruse that the patient had to ask him to print the letter.

Admonish: MEANING: Reprimand, warn

SENTENCE: She admonished him for pouring a third glass of wine.

Adulterate: MEANING: Debase a substance by adding another substance

SENTENCE: Cocaine is adulterated and dangerous.

Aesthetic: MEANING: Concerned with beauty

SENTENCE: There are practical as well as aesthetic reasons for planting trees; not only do trees give oxygen needed for human and animal life, but they also add beauty.

Affability: MEANING: A tendency to be friendly and approachable

SENTENCE: John's affability helped him in his interview with the Fulbright Scholarship decision panel; they selected him for the scholarship.

Affluent: MEANING: Wealthy, well off

SENTENCE: Judging by the size of the houses and the abundance of trees, this was an affluent suburb.

Aggrandize: MEANING: Increase in power, wealth, rank; or enlarge, e.g. aggrandize an estate.

SENTENCE: Some political leaders may aim to aggrandize their power without considering the wishes of their own political party.

Aggregate: MEANING: Gather into a mass or whole; accumulation of a whole

SENTENCE: The aggregate wealth of this country is staggering to the imagination.

Alacrity: MEANING: Speedy willingness

SENTENCE: He demonstrated his eagerness to cooperate by answering the email with alacrity.

Alleviate: MEANING: Lessen a problem or suffering

SENTENCE: The stimulus package has alleviated the problems of the Great Recession, but times are still tough.

Alluring: MEANING: Highly attractive, fascinating

SENTENCE: The music coming from the darkened bar was very alluring to the travellers.

Amalgam: MEANING: A mixture of multiple things

SENTENCE: The music played by the band was an amalgam of hip-hop, flamenco and jazz, blending the three styles with surprising results.

Ambiguous: MEANING: not clear or decided

SENTENCE: The election result was ambiguous.

Ambivalent: MEANING: having mixed emotions about something

SENTENCE: Sam was ambivalent about studying for the exam because doing so was time-consuming, yet he was able to improve his analytical skills.

Ameliorate: MEANING: To make better

SENTENCE: Isabel's pain of scoring less in the exam than Kate was ameliorated when she discovered she still qualified for the Fulbright Scholarship.

Anachronism: MEANING: An error in chronology; something out of date or old-fashioned

SENTENCE: it is an anachronism to see a horse and cart on the freeway.

Analogous: MEANING: Comparable, similar

SENTENCE: Living with a pet is analogous to having a young child; you have to watch what they put into their mouth.

Anarchy: MEANING: Absence of law or government

SENTENCE: Once the dictator was assassinated, the country fell into total anarchy, as none of the opposition groups were strong enough to seize power.

Anomaly: MEANING: Deviation from what is common; something which is unusual

SENTENCE: While the cosmetics division of the company has many female executives, it's an anomaly – in the rest of the company, sadly, only 4% of management positions are filled by women.

Antipathy: MEANING: A feeling of dislike or aversion

SENTENCE: There was widespread public antipathy towards inserting an identifying chip into the vaccine.

Antiquity: MEANING: Ancient times

SENTENCE: Gold antiquities were discovered in Pakistan; these belonged to some thousand years ago.

Apathy: MEANING: Lack of concern, motivation or interest in important matters

SENTENCE: As a firm believer in democratic government, she could not understand the apathy of people who never bothered to vote.

Appease: MEANING: Satisfy and relieve

SENTENCE: My mother is so angry she wasn't the first person we called when the baby was born – I'm hoping to appease her by bringing the baby to see her today!

Apprise: MEANING: Inform or tell (someone)

SENTENCE: I thought it was the right thing to apprise Chris of what had happened in his office while he was away.

Approbation: MEANING: approval or praise

SENTENCE: He wrote many approbations to works of Hebrew literature.

Appropriate: MEANING: suitable or proper in the circumstances

SENTENCE: It was entirely appropriate that she brought her boyfriend to the family Christmas party.

Arcane: MEANING: Secret, mysterious, known only to the initiated

SENTENCE: Cursive writing is becoming arcane in our world of word processing.

Arduous: MEANING: Requiring lots of hard work, very difficult

SENTENCE: Without a proper teacher, the exam is far too arduous to study for by yourself.

Articulate: MEANING: Using language in a clear, fluent way

SENTENCE: Her articulate presentation of the advertising campaign impressed her employers.

Artless: MEANING: Natural, without pretence or deception

SENTENCE: Many people believe that Imran Khan seems to be an artless politician who can eliminate corruption from Pakistan.

Ascetic: MEANING: Practising pronounced self-discipline from all forms of indulgence

SENTENCE: Religious people can live frugal and ascetic lives.

Assiduous: MEANING: Showing great care and perseverance

SENTENCE: She was assiduous in pointing out every feature of the home to the prospective buyers.

Assuage: MEANING: Provide relief from an unpleasant feeling

SENTENCE: The electricity supply finally resumed, and it assuaged the angry people; because after a few minutes they forgot their inconvenience.

Attenuate: MEANING: Reduce the force, effect, or value of

SENTENCE: Many people claim that the flu vaccine attenuates their illness.

Audacious: MEANING: Daring, bold; taking risks

SENTENCE: She made an audacious decision to quit her job.

Auspicious: MEANING: Favourable, positive

SENTENCE: The opening night of the musical received an auspicious review from the theatre critic.

Austere: MEANING: Severely simple, plain

SENTENCE: The graduation speaker Delivered an austere message: the economy Is bad, and academic success alone isn't enough to succeed in the job market.

Austerity: MEANING: Sternness, severity; reduced public spending

During the recession, the government introduced austerity measures, and many public servants were retrenched.

Autonomous: MEANING: Independent

SENTENCE: The country was comprised of a number of autonomous provinces.

Avarice: MEANING: Greed for wealth

SENTENCE: Early gold-diggers were inspired by avarice.

Avid: MEANING: Passionate or enthusiastic

SENTENCE: Hamid Is an avid reader of novels, articles and editorials; this helped his comprehension immensely.

-B -

Banal: MEANING: Lacking originality

SENTENCE: Frequent use of ordinary and uninteresting words makes an essay seem banal; this generates a low score in essays.

Belie: MEANING: Give a false impression

SENTENCE: The corrupt actions of some officials belie their claim to be representative of sound authority.

Beneficent: MEANING: (of a person) generous or doing good

SENTENCE: Clarissa found a beneficent mentor in her manager at work.

Benign: MEANING: Harmless

The doctor told Stephen that the lump on his arm was benign and could be removed easily.

Bracing: MEANING: Fresh, invigorating; giving strength

SENTENCE: Heather took her dog for a bracing walk by the ocean at 6am that day.

Burgeon: MEANING: Grow rapidly, flourish

SENTENCE: In the spring, the plants that burgeon are a promise of the beauty that is to come.

Burnish: MEANING: enhance or improve

SENTENCE: The politician took advantage of any opportunity to burnish his image.

Bolster: MEANING: Support or strengthen

SENTENCE: The fall in interest rates is starting to bolster investor confidence.

Bombastic: MEANING: Pompous, showy

SENTENCE: The speech made by the new headmaster was a little bombastic.

Boorish: MEANING: rough and bad-mannered; coarse.

SENTENCE: Even though the pirate captain was brutal and boorish with his men, he was always courteous to the female captives.

Buttress: MEANING: Support, reinforce

SENTENCE: In the debating club, the students learnt how to buttress their argument with relevant facts.

- C -

Cacophony: MEANING: A harsh, discordant, or meaningless mixture of sounds.

SENTENCE: The noise of barking dogs and sirens added to the cacophony at midnight; I didn't sleep.

Candid: MEANING: Sincere or honest

SENTENCE: The candid attitude of the prime minister inspired many young individuals to see him as a role model.

Capricious: MEANING: Unpredictable

SENTENCE: Share market behaviour was capricious during the COVID-19 pandemic.

Castigate: MEANING: Criticize harshly

SENTENCE: Drill sergeants are known to castigate new recruits so mercilessly that the latter often break down.

Chicanery: MEANING: The use of deception or subterfuge

SENTENCE: There is plenty of chicanery in the world of international espionage.

Catalyst: MEANING: Something that causes change

SENTENCE: The student's ideas were the catalyst for the teacher's different approach to teaching.

Caustic: MEANING: Intended to hurt, bitterly sarcastic

SENTENCE: The divorcing couple spoke to each other with caustic remarks.

Circumscribe: MEANING: Limit or restrict

SENTENCE: Unreliable access to funds circumscribed the investor's activities.

Coagulate: MEANING: (of a fluid) change to a solid or semi-solid state

SENTENCE: Blood had coagulated around the edges of the wound.

Chauvinism: MEANING: Excessive support for one's own cause, group or sex

SENTENCE: Male chauvinists do not believe women are their equal.

Coda: MEANING: A concluding event, section or remark

SENTENCE: A prayer was the coda to the priest's session that Sunday.

Cogent: MEANING: Convincing, logical

SENTENCE: The defence presented cogent arguments to the jury; their verdict: not guilty.

Commensurate: MEANING: Equal in extent, proportional

SENTENCE: Her salary was commensurate with her experience and qualifications.

Compendium: MEANING: a collection or set of similar items.

SENTENCE: The book she borrowed was a compendium of maps and stories of the country she planned to visit.

Complaisant: MEANING: Willing to please others

SENTENCE: Flight attendants are usually very complaisant with passengers.

Condone: MEANING: Accept or overlook behaviour that is considered wrong or offensive

SENTENCE: The school did not condone smoking in the playground.

Confound: MEANING: Cause confusion with surprise; mix up

SENTENCE: The twins would deliberately confound their teachers by swapping seats in the classroom.

Connoisseur: MEANING: Expert of art; or simply, expert

SENTENCE: Miguel managed a vineyard and was something of a wine connoisseur.

Compliant: MEANING: Submissive, willing to obey someone else

SENTENCE: He was compliant when the police asked him to step out of the car.

Contentious: MEANING: Likely to cause controversy

SENTENCE: The filmmaker produced a very contentious documentary on the state of the global environment.

Conciliatory: MEANING: Soothing and satisfying

SENTENCE: She was still angry despite his conciliatory words to her after their argument.

Contrite: MEANING: Feeling or expressing remorse

 SENTENCE: The teacher found a very contrite student when he visited the detention room.

Concomitant: MEANING: Accompanying, associated

SENTENCE: The joys of motherhood had concomitant anxieties.

Conundrum: MEANING: A difficult problem; puzzle

SENTENCE: The study of physics involved many conundrums.

Converge: MEANING: Tending to come together from different directions

SENTENCE: The crowd converged on the holy relic.

Convoluted: MEANING: Twisted, very complicated

SENTENCE: Your argument is so convoluted that I'm not able to understand it enough to start critiquing it.

Courteous: MEANING: Polite and respectful in manner

SENTENCE: The lawyer sent me a very courteous letter.

Craven: MEANING: Very cowardly

SENTENCE: When he saw the enemy troops advancing, he had a craven impulse to run for his life.

Crestfallen: MEANING: Dejected, sad and disappointed

SENTENCE: Half the crowd in the stadium were crestfallen after their team lost the grand final.

Culpability: MEANING: Deserving blame

SENTENCE: The extent of the culpability of each nation in its handling of the crisis became clearer over time.

Cursory: MEANING: Brief, hasty

SENTENCE: He gave the report a cursory glance before handing it to his secretary.

- D -

Dander: MEANING: Tiny particles, from hair, skin or feathers; a feeling of anger, temper

SENTENCE: The smirk on the villain's face raised the dander of the policeman.

Daunt: MEANING: Discourage or frighten

SENTENCE: The student daunted his classmate when the teacher was not looking.

Credulous: MEANING: Trusting too easily or without enough evidence.

SENTENCE: Few people are credulous enough to believe that the United Nations has global authority.

Debunk: MEANING: Show something to be false

SENTENCE: Investigative journalists have debunked various political myths.

Decorum: MEANING: Proper In manners and conduct

SENTENCE: Discipline requires the decorum of one's behaviour and attitude towards rules and regulations.

Default: MEANING: Failure to fulfil an obligation, especially a financial one

SENTENCE: The company will have to restructure its debts to avoid default.

Deference: MEANING: Polite and respectful submission

SENTENCE: He responded with natural deference, giving them his full attention.

Deliberation: MEANING: Careful consideration; slow movement

SENTENCE: The jury delivered its verdict after due deliberation.

Delineate: MEANING: Describe in precise detail

SENTENCE: I do need the cash, but I'm not signing up for this psychological experiment unless you delineate what's going to happen.

Demean: MEANING: Cause a loss in dignity and respect for something or someone; do something that is beneath one's dignity

SENTENCE: She did not demean herself by calling her boyfriend after seeing him with another girl.

Denigrate: MEANING: Criticize unfairly; disparage.

SENTENCE: Don't listen to the doom and gloom merchants who denigrate their own country.

Deride: MEANING: Express contempt for; ridicule.

SENTENCE: The decision to create a shopping mall in front of the lake was derided by environmentalists

Derivative: MEANING: Not original

SENTENCE: Many modern singers' albums are mere disappointment, derivative of several hit albums from past legends.

Desiccate: MEANING: Dehydrate, remove water from

SENTENCE: Out West, it was the time of the summer sun and dust storms, when whole desiccated farms blew away.

Desultory: MEANING: Lacking a plan, purpose, or enthusiasm

SENTENCE: A few people were left at the party, dancing in a desultory fashion.

Deterrent: MEANING: something that discourages or is intended to discourage someone from doing something

SENTENCE: Cameras are a major deterrent to crime

Diatribe: MEANING: A forceful and bitter verbal attack against someone or something

SENTENCE: The speech was a diatribe against consumerism.

Dichotomy: MEANING: A contrast between two things that are opposed, or very different.

SENTENCE: There is a fixed dichotomy between science and religion.

Didacticism: MEANING: A philosophy of teaching in art and literature

SENTENCE: The didactic qualities of his poetry overshadow its literary qualities; the lesson he teaches is more memorable than the lines.

Diffidence: MEANING: Lack of self-confidence, shyness

SENTENCE: Her diffidence showed up in the classroom when she was asked to speak.

Diffuse: MEANING: Spread out over a large area; not concentrated

SENTENCE: New technologies diffuse rapidly.

Digression: MEANING: a temporary departure from the main subject in speech or writing.

SENTENCE: "Let's return to the main topic after that brief digression."

Disabuse: MEANING: Free somebody from an incorrect belief.

SENTENCE: I will attempt to disabuse you of your impression of my client's guilt; I know he is innocent.

Discerning: MEANING: Mentally quick and observant

SENTENCE: The ships in the harbour were not discernible in the fog.

Discordant: MEANING: Disagreeing or incongruous; lacking in harmony

SENTENCE: The operative principle of democracy is a balance of discordant qualities

Discountenance: MEANING: Refuse to approve of; disturb the composure of

SENTENCE: When capitalist development discountenances the people, it loses its soul. The soul of capitalist development at the national, regional and global level must be the people.

Discredit: MEANING: Injure The reputation of

SENTENCE: the campaign was highly negative in tone; each candidate tried to discredit the other.

Discrepancy: MEANING: Lack of consistency between facts

SENTENCE: There is a discrepancy between the accountant's report and the client's.

Dirge: MEANING: A mournful song, piece of music, or sound

SENTENCE: When Kim sang a dirge for her deceased father, she brought everyone to tears.

Discrete: MEANING: Individually separate

SENTENCE: Speech is produced as a continuous sound signal rather than discrete units.

Disingenuous: MEANING: Not sincere, not simple

SENTENCE: Although he was young, his remarks indicated that he was disingenuous.

Disinterested: MEANING: Unprejudiced by consideration of personal gain; uninterested.

SENTENCE: My decision to invest in your company is a disinterested one; I am acting on behalf of a client.

Disjointed: MEANING: Disconnected

SENTENCE: In politics we have seen, whenever there is a clash of interests, political parties have become disjointed.

Dismiss: MEANING: Discharge from an office or position; treat as unworthy of consideration

SENTENCE: The prime minister dismissed five members of his cabinet.

Disparage: MEANING: Belittle, regard as being of little worth

SENTENCE: The feminist group tended to disparage men.

Disparate: MEANING: Essentially different, not able to be compared.

SENTENCE: The two authors inhabit disparate worlds of thought.

Disquieting: MEANING: Disturbing, causing anxiety.

SENTENCE: Mr. Amir's lack of emotion at his wife's death was disquieting – so much so, in fact, that even his own family began to suspect he had something to do with it.

Dissemble: MEANING: Hide or disguise one's real feelings or beliefs

SENTENCE: She smiled and looked away, dissembling her true emotions.

Disseminate: MEANING: Spread widely, especially information

SENTENCE: Health authorities should foster good practice by disseminating information

Dissolution: MEANING: the action of ceasing or dismissing an assembly, partnership, or official body

SENTENCE: The dissolution of their marriage after 20 years took place in a few minutes.

Dissonance: MEANING: lack of agreement or harmony, especially in music

SENTENCE: The meeting ended in uproar and dissonance.

Distend: MEANING: Swell or cause to swell by pressure from inside

SENTENCE: The abdomen distended rapidly.

Distil: MEANING: Remove impurities from, increase the concentration of

SENTENCE: You can't drink the water from the river, but you can distil it.

Divest: MEANING: Take something away from somebody

SENTENCE: The president was divested of his power to act and could no longer govern.

Doctrinaire: MEANING: Trying to impose doctrine without taking practical considerations into account

SENTENCE: Mr. Chief Justice is such a doctrinaire person that he will never compromise on the sentences he makes for terrorists.

Document: MEANING: Support with evidence; written piece

SENTENCE: In the analytical writing assessment, if you write an essay with well-documented examples, you should get a high score.

Dogmatic: MEANING: inclined to lay down principles as undeniably true

SENTENCE: She was not tempted to be too dogmatic about what she believed.

Dogmatism: MEANING: The tendency to be right all the time, with little consideration for others

SENTENCE: Mr. Jones shows an inflexible dogmatism when it comes to answering difficult questions.

Dormant: MEANING: Temporarily inactive

SENTENCE: The disease may remain dormant and undetected until it is transmitted to other fish.

Dupe: MEANING: Trick, deceive

SENTENCE: The manager was duped into hiring a criminal.

- E -

Ebullient: MEANING: Energetic and full of cheer

SENTENCE: Fatima sounded ebullient and happy when she got very high exam score.

Eccentric: MEANING: Odd; deviating from normal, unusual

SENTENCE: Her parents were eccentric but very lovable.

Eclectic: MEANING: Selecting what seems best from various styles or ideas

SENTENCE: The government applied a set of bipartisan and eclectic policies.

Efficacy: MEANING: The quality of being able to produce the intended effect

SENTENCE: The efficacy of your preparation of the exam depends on your devotion and hard work.

Effrontery: MEANING: Rude or impertinent behaviour

SENTENCE: The teacher condones no effrontery in her classroom.

Egregious: MEANING: Extremely bad to such an extent that it becomes shocking

SENTENCE: The prime minister's abuse of power was so egregious that even his own family deserted him and asked the international courts to take action against him.

Elegy: MEANING: a mournful poem; a lament for the dead

SENTENCE: An example of an elegy is a poem written to honour a deceased man

Elicit: MEANING: Draw out a reaction, answer, or fact

SENTENCE: I tried to elicit a smile from Joanna.

Eloquence: MEANING: Persuasive speech or writing

SENTENCE: She spoke with such eloquence at the meeting.

Embellish: MEANING: Decorate and adorn; add details to a story that may not be accurate

SENTENCE: My mother-in-law's stories about her journey from Russia made us laugh because she embellished the bare facts of her travels with humorous anecdotes.

Empirical: MEANING: Based on experience or experimentation

SENTENCE: He distrusted hunches and intuitive flashes; he placed his reliance entirely on empirical data.

Emulate: MEANING: Imitate; match or surpass by imitation

SENTENCE: Many singers wished to emulate Elvis Presley.

Endemic: MEANING:) Regularly found among particular people or in a certain area (of a disease or condition)

SENTENCE: Is surging inequality endemic to capitalism?

Enervate: MEANING: To weaken physically, mentally or morally

SENTENCE: The long suffering from paralysis has enervated him.

Engender: MEANING: Give rise to, cause (a feeling, situation, or condition)

SENTENCE: The issue of race raised by the politician has engendered continuing controversy.

Enhance: MEANING: Further improve the quality, value, or extent of; intensify, increase

SENTENCE: His refusal does nothing to enhance his reputation.

Ephemeral: MEANING: Lasting only a short time

SENTENCE: The mayfly is an ephemeral creature; it only lives for a couple of hours.

Equanimity: MEANING: Calmness and composure, especially in difficult situations

SENTENCE: She accepted both the good and the bad with equanimity.

Equitable: MEANING: Impartial or fair

SENTENCE: The mediator suggested an equitable solution for both parties.

Equivocate: MEANING: To speak vaguely so as to conceal the truth

SENTENCE: After Sharon brought the car home an hour after her curfew, she equivocated when her parents pointedly asked her where she had been.

Erroneous: MEANING: Wrong, incorrect

SENTENCE: I thought my answer was correct, but it was erroneous; it's usually the case for tricky questions.

Erudite: MEANING: Well-educated, having or showing great knowledge or learning

SENTENCE: Steve turned any conversation into an erudite discussion.

Esoteric: MEANING: Understood by only a few people with specialized knowledge or interests; obscure

SENTENCE: She read a compilation of esoteric philosophical theories.

Eulogy: MEANING: Expression of praise, often on the occasion of someone's death.

SENTENCE: All the eulogies of his friends were read in church and the funeral was attended by many.

Euphemism: MEANING: an expression substituted for one considered to be too blunt when referring to something unpleasant or embarrassing

SENTENCE: The phrase 'passed away' is a euphemism for saying someone died.

Euphoria: MEANING: A feeling of extreme excitement

SENTENCE: Katie was euphoric after she got an admission at Harvard University, with full scholarship.

Exacerbate: MEANING: Make worse

SENTENCE: The cream the doctor prescribed only exacerbated the rash on Steve's foot.

Exacting: MEANING: Extremely demanding

SENTENCE: The author's requirements were exacting, the editor would need weeks to do the work.

Exculpate: MEANING: Show someone is free from blame

SENTENCE: I will present evidence of innocence and honesty in his 10 years of service for this country that will exculpate my client from such groundless charges.

Exigency: MEANING: Urgent requirement or need

SENTENCE: Political decisions are presented as a matter of exigency, as though there were no other choice.

Exonerate: MEANING: Officially absolve from blame; release from obligation or duty

SENTENCE: In order to work in the USA, one requires proof of exoneration from any criminal act.

Extraneous: MEANING: Irrelevant; of external origin

SENTENCE: We create bubbles of information, silos of opinion, and we tune out all that is extraneous or disagreeable.

Extrapolation: MEANING: The action of estimating by extension of current trends, or applying current methods

SENTENCE: I extrapolate that getting home will take 20 minutes as it took 20 minutes to get there.

- F -

Facetious: MEANING: Inappropriately funny, flippant

SENTENCE: Facetious remarks about a classmate are inappropriate at the serious moment when you got an excellent score in the exam, but your classmate got a very poor score.

Facile: MEANING: Superficial, simplistic; easily achieved

SENTENCE: His essay contained many facile generalizations.

Facilitate: MEANING: Make an action or process easier.

SENTENCE: Businesses were located in the same area to facilitate the residents' visiting and shopping.

Fallacious: MEANING: Based on unsound arguments

SENTENCE: Don't be misled by the fallacious advertisement.

Faltering: MEANING: Hesitating; losing strength or momentum

SENTENCE: The surprising decrease in the value of the euro as compared to other currencies is sign of a faltering economy.

Fastidious: MEANING: Giving very careful attention to detail

SENTENCE: The Professor is so fastidious that he hardly ever approves a student's thesis on first submission, because he is so fastidious about little points like punctuation.

Fatuous: MEANING: Silly, foolish

SENTENCE: Her comments on the film festival competition were fatuous.

Fawning: MEANING: Showing exaggerated affection or flattery; obsequious

SENTENCE: The puppy was fawning on its master.

Felicitous: MEANING: Apt, suited to the circumstances; pleasing

SENTENCE: The felicitous music made me happy.

Fervor: MEANING: Intense and earnest feeling

SENTENCE: The priest delivered his sermon with great fervor.

Flag: MEANING: Lose enthusiasm or energy

SENTENCE: When the opposing hockey team scored its third goal only minutes into the first period, the home team's spirits flagged.

Fledgling: MEANING: a person, creature or organization that is immature, inexperienced, or underdeveloped

SENTENCE: Pakistan is a country with a fledgling democracy

Flout: MEANING: Openly disregard, in terms of a rule, law, or convention

SENTENCE: They hugged each other, openly flouting the social distancing rules.

Foible: MEANING: Slight flaw or defect, especially of character

SENTENCE: Her tendency to gossip was an all-too-human foible.

Foment: MEANING: To instigate or stir up, especially discord or trouble

SENTENCE: Greenpeace fomented protests on the ocean against whaling.

Forestall: MEANING: To prevent, hinder or thwart by action in advance

SENTENCE: They will hand in their resignations to forestall a vote of no confidence.

Forlorn: MEANING: Sad And lonely

SENTENCE: After his lover left him and went with some other guy, Edward was forlorn.

Fortuitous: MEANING: Occurring by happy chance; by lucky accident

SENTENCE: There is no connection between these two events; their timing is entirely fortuitous.

Frugality: MEANING: The attitude of not spending much money

SENTENCE: Monte was no miser, but was simply frugal, wisely spending the little that he earned.

Futile: MEANING: Useless, ineffective

SENTENCE: His attempts at scaling the wall were futile, it was simply too high for him.

- G -

Gainsay: MEANING: Deny or dispute; oppose

SENTENCE: He shrugged his shoulders, unable to gainsay the argument.

Galling: MEANING: Causing irritation, exasperating

SENTENCE: Learning vocabulary lists without sentence examples Is a galling thing for most students.

Gambit: MEANING: Action aimed at producing a future advantage; a remark to open or redirect a conversation

SENTENCE: One gambit is to require photo identification. This should ensure tenants are properly managed.

Garrulous: MEANING: Talkative, wordy

SENTENCE: Many club members avoided the company of the garrulous junior executive, because his constant chatter bored them to tears.

Gauche: MEANING: Clumsy and awkward in social behaviour

SENTENCE: It Is terribly gauche to put ketchup on your steak and then talk with your mouth full as you eat it! That's the last time I ever bring you to a nice place!

Gawky: MEANING: Physically awkward

SENTENCE: As a teenager, she thought of herself as gawky and often slouched so as not to seem so much taller than her peers; of course, now that she's a supermodel, no one thinks of her as gawky at all.

Glib: MEANING: Fluent with insincerity or superficiality

SENTENCE: Politicians are usually glib and articulate speakers; this helps them in their campaign.

Gloating: MEANING: Smug or malicious satisfaction

SENTENCE: After the fight, the winner stood over his opponent and gloated.

Goad: MEANING: Prod, incite, so as to stimulate an action or reaction.

SENTENCE: He was trying to goad her into a fight.

Gouge: MEANING: To scoop out and make grooves or holes

SENTENCE: The water channel had been gouged out by the ebbing water

Grandiloquent: MEANING: Expressed in lofty language, style, or manner, especially in a way that is intended to impress.

SENTENCE: The fiesta was a grandiloquent celebration of Spanish glory.

Gregarious: MEANING: Sociable, friendly

SENTENCE: As a gregarious boy Dave ran up to every person on the playground and wanted to be their friend.

Grovelling: MEANING: Behaving in a fawning or servile manner

SENTENCE: Journalists like to describe political leaders as grovelling in their interactions with others.

Guileless: MEANING: Innocent and without deception

SENTENCE: The student gave a guileless explanation of his absence from class.

Gullible: MEANING: Easily persuaded to believe something; credulous

SENTENCE: The plan was a deliberate attempt to persuade a gullible public to spend their money.

- H -

Hackneyed: MEANING: Commonplace, not fresh or original

SENTENCE: The English teacher criticized her story because of its hackneyed and unoriginal plot.

Halcyon: MEANING: Calm; rich; happy

SENTENCE: There were halcyon days all summer.

Harangue: MEANING: A long verbal attack; pompous speech

SENTENCE: The speaker on the soapbox harangued the government.

Harrowing: MEANING: Extremely disturbing or distressing

SENTENCE: The trip in the ambulance was harrowing for them both.

Hodgepodge: MEANING: Jumble of different kinds of things

SENTENCE: The exhibition was a hodgepodge of mediocre art, bad art, and really bad art; it was disliked by many visitors.

Homogeneous: MEANING: of the same kind; alike

SENTENCE: The unemployed are not a homogenous group.

Humdrum: MEANING: Boring, monotonous, routine

SENTENCE: After five years in the same role, Sandra found the work a little humdrum.

Hyperbole: MEANING: Exaggeration

SENTENCE: Oh, come on, saying 'that movie was so bad it made me puke,' was surely hyperbole. I strongly doubt that you actually vomited!

Iconoclastic: MEANING: Defying tradition

SENTENCE: Jackson Pollack was an iconoclastic artist, totally breaking with tradition by splashing paint on a blank canvas.

Idolatry: MEANING: The worship of idols; excessive admiration

SENTENCE: We must not allow our idolatry of pop stars to make them seem more than mortal.

Ignominious: MEANING: Embarrassing, humiliating

SENTENCE: He suffered an ignominious defeat.

Immutable: MEANING: Unchanging over time, permanent

SENTENCE: Science presents us with some immutable facts, like gravity on planet Earth.

Impair: MEANING: Make worse, damage

SENTENCE: Listening to loud music without earplugs with almost certainly impair your hearing over time.

Impassive: MEANING: Not showing emotion

SENTENCE: His cold, impassive face stared at the cripple begging on the street.

Impede: MEANING: Block or obstruct progress

SENTENCE: The judge determined that the detective had not intentionally set out to impede the progress of the investigation.

Impermeable: MEANING: Not allowing fluid to pass through, waterproof

SENTENCE: The boat is made from impermeable wood.

Imperturbable: MEANING: Unshakeably calm

SENTENCE: Greg remained imperturbable during his exam, even the last moments before completion didn't panic him.

Impervious: MEANING: Not affected or influenced; resistant to water or heat

SENTENCE: The system remained impervious to all suggestions of change.

Implacable: MEANING: Hostile, unable to be appeased, relentless

SENTENCE: The barrister was implacable in his handling of the offence.

Implicit: MEANING: Not directly expressed; essentially connected with; absolute

SENTENCE: She had an implicit faith in God.

Implode: MEANING: Burst Inward

SENTENCE: There is a new technology of controlled demolition during which old buildings implode in a matter of seconds, without any damage to nearby buildings.

Inadvertently: MEANING: Accidentally, without intention

SENTENCE: Chris inadvertently dialled Sandra's number and she happily answered the call.

Incensed: MEANING: Extremely angry

SENTENCE: Mr. Smith is known for his kindness towards children; unkindness towards children by others incensed him.

Incessantly: MEANING: Continuing without stopping

SENTENCE: The batsman hit boundaries and sixes incessantly and won the game!

Inchoate: MEANING: Just begun, not fully developed; rudimentary

SENTENCE: The country was a still inchoate democracy.

Incongruity: MEANING: Mismatch; incompatibility

SENTENCE: The incongruity of his fleshy face and skinny body disturbed her.

Inconsequential: MEANING: Having little importance; illogical; haphazard

SENTENCE: Her answers were inconsequential despite the numbering on the page.

Incorporate: MEANING: Bring something into a larger whole; include

SENTENCE: The second division team incorporated third division players in the latter half of the season.

Incorrigible: MEANING: A person or behaviour that cannot be reformed or changed

SENTENCE: My friend's father is an incorrigible drinker.

Indefatigable: MEANING: Tirelessly persisting

SENTENCE: He had courage, a vivid sense of duty, an indefatigable love of work, and all the inquisitive zeal and inventive energy of a born reformer.

Indeterminate: MEANING: Vague and unclear, cannot be determined

SENTENCE: Our galaxy has an indeterminate number of stars

Indifferent: MEANING: Not caring, unconcerned; mediocre

SENTENCE: Because she felt no desire to marry, she was indifferent to the constant proposals by her lover.

Indigence: MEANING: A state of extreme poverty; destitution

SENTENCE: After the U.S. Supreme Court case, Gideon v. Wainwright in 1963, state governments were required to provide lawyers to indigent defendants.

Indolent: MEANING: Lazy, wanting to avoid effort or exertion

SENTENCE: At lunchtime the indolent kids sat around while the active kids played games.

Ineluctable: MEANING: Inescapable, unable to be avoided

SENTENCE: Two ineluctable facts of life are death and taxes.

Inert: MEANING: Not able to move; inactive

SENTENCE: The story was inert and careless, as if the author was writing half-asleep.

Inexorable: MEANING: Continuing without any possibility of being stopped

SENTENCE: Technology moves inexorably towards a digital future.

Inherent: MEANING: Existing as a permanent, essential quality

SENTENCE: New research seems to support the idea that humans have an inherent sense of fairness – even babies become upset at equal and unequal distributions of food.

Innocuous: MEANING: Harmless, inoffensive

SENTENCE: The journalist asked a couple of innocuous questions at the press conference.

Insatiable: MEANING: Unable to be satisfied, physically and spiritually

SENTENCE: She has an insatiable desire to learn the English language.

Inscrutability: MEANING: The quality of being impossible to investigate

SENTENCE: There is a certain inscrutability of the future.

Insensible: MEANING: Barely able to be perceived; incapable of sensation

SENTENCE: There was an insensible change in his temperature.

Insinuate: MEANING: Hint at something negative; become involved in a subtle way

SENTENCE: He insinuated himself into the conversation of the people at the nearby table.

Insipid: MEANING: Lacking flavour, weak or tasteless

SENTENCE: The first band to play at the concert was a little insipid.

Insularity: MEANING: The quality of being isolated or detached

SENTENCE: The 1950s were a decade of conservatism and insularity.

Intractable: MEANING: Difficult to manage or mould

SENTENCE: The kindergarten kids were intractable and the teacher grew frustrated.

Intransigence: MEANING: Unwillingness to change one' beliefs; stubbornness

SENTENCE: Despite many calls for mercy, the judge remained intransigent, citing strict legal precedence.

Inundate: MEANING: Quickly fill up, overwhelm

SENTENCE: Her inbox was inundated with emails on her birthday.

Inured: MEANING: Made tough by habitual exposure

SENTENCE: He was inured to the sound of his neighbour's dog barking.

Invective: MEANING: Insulting, abusive, or highly critical language

SENTENCE: His invective was overheard by everyone in the next office.

Involved: MEANING: Connected; highly complex

SENTENCE: She was involved in animal care through her Girl Guides membership.

Irascible: MEANING: Having or showing a tendency to be easily angered.

SENTENCE: Early in their marriage, Julie discovered her husband could be irascible.

Irresolute: MEANING: Uncertain how to act or proceed

SENTENCE: The new governor was irresolute; he needed the advice from the committee.

Itinerary: MEANING: A planned route or journey

SENTENCE: His itinerary included an official visit to Canada

- L -

Lacklustre: MEANING: Lacking energy, excitement, enthusiasm, or passion.

SENTENCE: We were disappointed by the lacklustre performance of our cricket team this weekend.

Laconic: MEANING: Saying very little

SENTENCE: While Martha always swooned over the hunky, laconic types in romantic comedies, her boyfriend was very talkative – and not very hunky.

Largesse: MEANING: Liberality in bestowing gifts; generous of spirit

SENTENCE: Her partner's largesse warmed her heart; he was generous to family, friends and neighbours.

Lassitude: MEANING: Tiredness, laziness

SENTENCE: As a couch potato I turn lassitude into an art form!

Latent: MEANING: Existing, but not yet developed or manifest; hidden or concealed.

SENTENCE: Australia has a huge reserve of latent talent.

Laud: MEANING: Praise highly

SENTENCE: In the newspaper obituary, she was lauded as a brilliant opera singer.

Lethargic: MEANING: Affected by lethargy; sluggish and apathetic

SENTENCE: Yesterday I felt lethargic and stayed at home; today I am rearing to go!

Levee: MEANING: An embankment built to prevent the overflow of a river

SENTENCE: They had their picnic on the levee next to the river.

Levity: MEANING: Lacking seriousness

SENTENCE: Stop giggling and wriggling around in the pew; such levity is improper in church.

Log: MEANING: Record of day-to-day activities; tree trunk

SENTENCE: Lawyers who bill by the hour have to be sure to log all the time they spend on every client's case.

Loquacious: MEANING: Talkative, wordy.

SENTENCE: MIguel is very loquacious and can speak on the telephone for hours.

Lucid: MEANING: Easily understood; clear; intelligible.

SENTENCE: Example sentences are another lucid way of learning vocabulary.

Lull: MEANING: Cause to fall asleep; quieten down

SENTENCE: The continuous reading of vocabulary lulled Miriam to sleep.

Luminous: MEANING: Giving off soft light; shining

SENTENCE: Her happy face was luminous in the twilight.

- M -

Magnanimity: MEANING: Generosity of spirit; unselfishness

SENTENCE: Both sides will have to show magnanimity to reach a compromise.

Maladroit: MEANING: Not skilful; awkward; bungling

SENTENCE: A maladroit movement of his hands caused the car to swerve.

Malfeasance: MEANING: Wrongdoing by a public official

SENTENCE: The high-ranking official's malfeasance was discovered only after he had fled the country.

Malingerer: MEANING: Someone who shirks duty, work or effort, often pretending to be unwell

SENTENCE: The doctor said my son was a malingerer.

Malleable: MEANING: Easily influenced; pliable

SENTENCE: The fans of the governor are as malleable and easily led as sheep.

Maverick: MEANING: Rebel, nonconformist

SENTENCE: Most cop movies feature heroes that are maverick police officers, breaking all the rules, blowing things up, and getting their guns confiscated by the chief – but ultimately saving the day.

Mawkish: MEANING: Effusively or insincerely emotional; excessively sentimental

SENTENCE: The Valentine's Day cards were a bit mawkish to my taste.

Mellifluous: MEANING: Pleasing to the ear

SENTENCE: Ali woke up early to the mellifluous singing of sparrows.

Mendacious: MEANING: Not telling the truth; lying.

SENTENCE: The political party workers had been mendacious throughout the court investigation and as a result they were punished severely.

Mendacity: MEANING: The tendency to be untruthful

SENTENCE: You need to overcome this deplorable mendacity, or no one will ever believe anything you say.

Metamorphosis: MEANING: Change of form or shape.

SENTENCE: The metamorphosis of caterpillar to butterfly is typical of many such changes in animal life.

Meticulous: MEANING: Extremely careful and precise

SENTENCE: She was meticulous in her proofreading and copy-editing business.

Mimicking: MEANING: Copying, imitating

SENTENCE: When Richard was caught mimicking his teacher in a rude way, he was put on detention.

Misanthrope: MEANING: A person who dislikes humankind and avoids human society.

SENTENCE: Hostile and untrusting people can be described as misanthropic.

Mitigate: MEANING: Lessen the extent of a harmful or negative outcome

SENTENCE: Sunscreen is used to mitigate the effects of sun on your skin.

Modicum: MEANING: A small or moderate amount

SENTENCE: When you awarded the Fulbright Scholarship, you will have only a modicum expense of the visa to bear; all major expenses are covered by the scholarship.

Mollify: MEANING: Calm or soothe; gain the good will of

SENTENCE: We tried to mollify the hysterical child by promising her many gifts.

Morbid: MEANING: Suggesting the horror of death and decay

SENTENCE: The stories of the war were morbid and upsetting to the children.

Morose: MEANING: Extremely gloomy and depressed

SENTENCE: She was morose after her aunt passed away.

Mundane: MEANING: Common, ordinary

SENTENCE: He was concerned only with mundane matters; where to park the car, what butcher was best etc.

- N -

Nascent: MEANING: The birth or beginning of something

SENTENCE: If we could identify these revolutionary movements in their nascent state, we would be able to eliminate serious trouble in later years.

Negate: MEANING: Make ineffective by counterbalancing the effect of

SENTENCE: The discovery of one dinosaur jaw negated the wisdom that all dinosaurs were vegetarian; that jaw was from a carnivore.

Nuance: MEANING: Shade of subtle difference in meaning, colour or feeling;

SENTENCE: The unskilled eye of the layperson has difficulty in discerning the nuances of colour in the painting.

- O -

Obdurate: MEANING: Stubborn

SENTENCE: I argued this point with him, but he was obdurate despite all the convincing reasons I could give.

Objurgation: MEANING: Harsh criticism

SENTENCE: When someone receives a severe scolding, they experience objurgation.

Neophyte: MEANING: A person who is brand new to a subject or activity

SENTENCE: Four-day cooking classes are offered to both neophytes and experts.

Nettlesome: MEANING: Causing irritation or annoyance; easily annoyed

SENTENCE: She found the paperwork in her job very nettlesome.

Notoriety: MEANING: Famous but for negative reasons

SENTENCE: The notoriety of Pakistan as a corrupt state is due to its lack of a genuine system for accountability.

Obsequious: MEANING: Servile, fawning

SENTENCE: The famous singer had an entourage of friends and staff, many of whom were obsequious.

Obviate: MEANING: Eliminate a need or difficulty

SENTENCE: To obviate an ant infestation we clean our kitchen regularly.

Occlude: MEANING: Close up, or obstruct (an opening)

SENTENCE: Foundation make-up occludes the pores of our skin.

Officious: MEANING: Excessively eager in giving unwanted advice, interfering

SENTENCE: My colleague can be officious in telling me how to do my job. It is annoying!

Omniscience: MEANING: All-knowing; having infinite knowledge

SENTENCE: Nobody except God can claim to have omniscience.

Onerous: MEANING: Involving a great deal of effort, trouble, or difficulty

SENTENCE: He found his duties increasingly onerous.

Opprobrium: MEANING: A state of extreme dishonour

SENTENCE: He threw a can of drink off the balcony, and earnt opprobrium.

Orthodox: MEANING: Traditional; adhering to what is commonly accepted

SENTENCE: He was an orthodox vegetarian; he did not even eat fish.

Ostentatious: MEANING: Characterized by a pretentious or showy display; designed to impress

SENTENCE: Her dress was a simple design – glamorous without being ostentatious.

- P -

Paradigm: MEANING: Standard example; accepted perspective

SENTENCE: Far from being atypically bawdy, this limerick is a paradigm of the form – nearly all of them rely on off-colour jokes.

Paragon: MEANING: A person or thing regarded as a perfect example of a particular quality.

SENTENCE: My mother was the paragon of kindness; she was beloved by many.

Partisan: MEANING: One-sided; prejudiced

SENTENCE: Our judicial system consists of partisan judges; in order to be promoted as a judge, one should have a strong relationship with a strong political party.

Pathological: MEANING: Caused by physical or mental disease

SENTENCE: Her friend turned out to be a pathological liar, nothing she ever said was true.

Patronising: MEANING: Treating others with condescension

SENTENCE: Experts in a field sometimes appear to patronise people who are less knowledgeable on the subject.

Paucity: MEANING: The presence of something in only small or insufficient quantities

SENTENCE: A paucity of good cheer at the party led to the host turning up the music.

Pedantic: MEANING: Excessively concerned with minor details or rules; overly scrupulous

SENTENCE: His analyses are careful and even painstaking, but never pedantic.

Pedestrian: MEANING: Ordinary; dull

SENTENCE: Vocabulary class without example sentences looks to be pedestrian for many students.

Penchant: MEANING: Liking, preference or strong inclination

SENTENCE: He had a strong penchant for sculpture and owned so many statues.

Perfidious: MEANING: Untrustworthy and deceitful

SENTENCE: The lawyer decided not to represent his perfidious client.

Perfunctory: MEANING: Done routinely and with little interest or care

SENTENCE: Her boyfriend gave her a perfunctory kiss on his way out the door.

Peripheral: MEANING: Not of primary importance

SENTENCE: My main goal is to get into a good graduate school; whether it has good fitness facilities is really a peripheral concern.

Permeable: MEANING: Allowing liquids or gases to pass through

SENTENCE: A frog's skin is permeable to water.

Perspicacious: MEANING: Shrewd, wise, discerning

SENTENCE: For a five-year-old kid, Toby was very perspicacious.

Penury: MEANING: Extreme poverty

SENTENCE: A job loss and family breakdown can lead to penury.

Perennial: MEANING: Lasting for an infinite time; enduring or continually recurring

SENTENCE: His parents had a perennial distrust of the media.

Pervasive: MEANING: Spreading or spread throughout, everywhere

SENTENCE: Talking about the weather is pervasive among adults.

Phlegmatic: MEANING: Having an unemotional and stolidly calm disposition.

SENTENCE: The British character can be phlegmatic compared with the emotional Spanish.

Phony: MEANING: Fake; insincere

SENTENCE: She's such a phony person, pretending to befriend people and then talking about them behind their backs.

Piety: MEANING: Devotion to God or to religious practices.

SENTENCE: The nuns live lives of piety and charitable works.

Placate: MEANING: Pacify; bring peace to

SENTENCE: The teacher tried to placate the upset mother whose child had failed in the class.

Placid: MEANING: Peaceful, calm

SENTENCE: Her dog was quite placid, and did not struggle when the vet gave him an injection.

Plasticity: MEANING: The quality of being easily shaped or moulded

SENTENCE: Fine clay, at the right degree of plasticity, is more useful.

Plethora: MEANING: An abundance or excess or something

SENTENCE: She had a plethora of potential dates; 10 boys asked her out.

Plummet: MEANING: Drop sharply; fall straight down.

SENTENCE: During the first minute or so of a skydive, the diver plummets towards earth in free fall; then, he activates a parachute and floats down at what seems like a relatively leisurely pace.

Polemical: MEANING: Involving controversy or dispute

SENTENCE: Don't discuss politics with your parents; it will only end up in a polemical argument.

Porous: MEANING: Full of holes or openings

SENTENCE: The border between the USA and Mexico was porous before they built the wall.

Pragmatic: MEANING: A person or solution that takes a realistic approach

SENTENCE: My daughter wants a unicorn for her birthday, which isn't very pragmatic.

Platitude: MEANING: A trite or obvious remark; a cliche

SENTENCE: The pep talk the boss gave to his team was full of platitudes.

Preamble: MEANING: Introductory statement, preface

SENTENCE: His early publications were just a preamble to his later, extensive written works.

Preclude: MEANING: Prevent from happening, make impossible

SENTENCE: Taking the Pill precluded her from falling pregnant.

Precariously: MEANING: Dangerously

SENTENCE: The glass was precariously balanced on the edge of the table.

Precipitate: MEANING: cause something to happen suddenly, unexpectedly and not always in a good way

SENTENCE: The assassination of the Archbishop precipitated World War Two.

Prevarication: MEANING: The deliberate act of deviating from the truth

SENTENCE: The reporter said that he is extremely sorry for spreading the prevarications about the Prime Minister's death in the hospital.

Pristine: MEANING: Unspoiled; remaining in a pure state

SENTENCE: Much of the coastline of Australia is made up of pristine beaches.

Precursor: MEANING: Something that comes before, and indicates that something will follow

SENTENCE: Pride is a precursor to a fall.

Probity: MEANING: The quality of having strong moral principles; honesty and decency

SENTENCE: She showed great probity in the divorce process and they split amicably.

Prescient: MEANING: Having or showing knowledge of events before they take place

SENTENCE: It is difficult, now, to appreciate just how prescient her art work was.

Problematic: MEANING: Constituting or presenting a problem.

SENTENCE: The COVID-19 lockdown was problematic for businesses and employees.

Presumptuous: MEANING: Taking liberties, bold forwardness

SENTENCE: I hope I won't be considered presumptuous if I offer you some advice.

Prodigal: MEANING: Rashly or wastefully extravagant

SENTENCE: Out of all the family, their uncle was the most prodigal, and they bailed him out frequently.

Profound: MEANING: Very insightful; deep

SENTENCE: She realised the book offered some very profound messages on our current society.

Prevaricate: MEANING: Be deliberately ambiguous in order to mislead

SENTENCE: His style was to prevaricate, but she saw through him and got to the truth.

Prohibitive: MEANING: Tending to discourage (especially prices)

SENTENCE: The books were made browser-proof with prohibitive cellophane wrapping.

Proliferate: MEANING: Increase rapidly in number; multiply

SENTENCE: Science fiction magazines proliferated in the 1920s.

Prolific: MEANING: Productive; fruitful

SENTENCE: She wrote three songs before breakfast; she was a prolific songwriter in this stage of her career.

Propensity: MEANING: An inclination or natural tendency to behave in a particular way

SENTENCE: The dog has a propensity to bark, and we have a propensity to be annoyed by it!

Proscribe: MEANING: Forbid, especially by law

SENTENCE: The headmaster proscribed the use of mobile phones in the classroom.

Protracted: MEANING: Drawn out for a long time, in a tedious way

SENTENCE: The protracted heat had the effect of driving people away from the city yesterday.

Prudent: MEANING: Wise; judicious.

SENTENCE: Her partner was prudent with their money and their future, which made her very happy!

Punctiliously: MEANING: Fastidiously, very carefully

SENTENCE: British soldiers act punctiliously at the changing of the guard at Buckingham Palace.

Propitiate: MEANING: win or regain favour; appease

SENTENCE: He propitiated his mother on Mother's Day with a bouquet and a box of chocolates.

Pungent: MEANING: Having a sharply strong taste or smell

SENTENCE: This homegrown garlic has a particularly pungent flavour.

Propriety: MEANING: Conforming to good manners or appropriate behaviour

SENTENCE: They questioned the propriety of certain investments made by the council.

- Q -

Qualified: MEANING: officially recognized as being trained to perform a particular job; certified

SENTENCE: I was well qualified with a degree to teach the class English vocabulary!

Quibble: MEANING: Small fight or argument over something unimportant

SENTENCE: She did not want to quibble over a few euros when she bought the dog from the pet shop.

Quiescent: MEANING: Resting, quiet

SENTENCE: He enjoyed quiescent moments in his garden hammock on a beautiful summer Sunday.

Quotidian: MEANING: Daily, routine, ordinary

SENTENCE: She enjoyed all things quotidian: doing chores, brushing her teeth, going to work, because she had a happy nature.

- R -

Rankle: MEANING: Aggravate; make angry

SENTENCE: We did not want to rankle the cat, so we put the puppy outside.

Rarefied: MEANING: Elevated above the ordinary

SENTENCE: The scholars were in an animated and rarefied conversation about world politics.

Rebuttal: MEANING: A counter argument to argument; a disagreement

SENTENCE: Steve rebutted Jason's view that his team would win the game.

Recalcitrant: MEANING: Obstinately uncooperative; pig-headed

SENTENCE: She has a class of recalcitrant fifteen-year-olds.

Recant: MEANING: Take back something that was previously said

SENTENCE: Heretics were burned if they did not recant.

Recluse: MEANING: A person who lives a solitary life and tends to avoid other people

SENTENCE: After returning from the pilgrimage she has turned into a virtual recluse.

Recondite: MEANING: Difficult to comprehend; abstruse

SENTENCE: The book on mathematical theory is full of recondite information.

Refractory: MEANING: Stubborn or unmanageable

SENTENCE: My dog is refractory on the lead; he does not want to walk!

Refute: MEANING: Prove to be false

SENTENCE: She refuted her kids' claim they had brushed their teeth by producing the dry toothbrushes.

Relegate: MEANING: Assign to an inferior rank or position

SENTENCE: Their soccer team was relegated to third division in the new season.

Reproach: MEANING: Criticize.

SENTENCE: I want my work to be above reproach and without error

Reprobate: MEANING: An unprincipled person; a bad egg

SENTENCE: The politician had to present himself as more of a lovable reprobate than a purely corrupt official.

Repudiate: MEANING: Refuse to accept; reject.

SENTENCE: As an adult, Ben repudiated the religion of his upbringing and went to work on Sundays.

Rescind: MEANING: Revoke, cancel, or repeal (a law, order, or agreement)

SENTENCE: The government eventually rescinded the policy after it faced severe criticism from both the opposition and the public.

Resolution: MEANING: Quality of being firmly determined

SENTENCE: Given the many areas of conflict still awaiting resolution, the outcome of the peace talks remains problematic.

Resolve: MEANING: Settle or find a solution to a problem or contentious matter

SENTENCE: The firm aims to resolve problems within 30 days

Reticent: MEANING: Quiet, restrained

SENTENCE: She was reticent about her feelings in his company as she did not know him very well.

Revelling: MEANING: Taking great pleasure

SENTENCE: After receiving the job offer she revelled all weekend with her family and friends.

Reverent: MEANING: Feeling or showing deep and solemn respect

SENTENCE: In church there is a reverent silence when the priest says, 'Let us pray.'

Rudimentary: MEANING: Basic; crude

SENTENCE: The test will be easy; it only requires a rudimentary knowledge of English.

- S -

Sagacious: MEANING: Acutely wise, very shrewd

SENTENCE: The president acquired some sagacious advisors to help him with managing the economy.

Sage: MEANING: A profoundly wise man, especially in ancient history or legend

SENTENCE: Aristotle, the great Athenian philosopher, was undoubtedly a sage.

Salubrious: MEANING: Conducive to health or wellbeing

SENTENCE: After spending many years smoking and drinking, Tom recognized the necessity of adopting a more salubrious lifestyle.

Sanction: MEANING: Approve, give permission; punish, speak harshly to

SENTENCE: America's sanctions on Cuba mean that it is illegal for Americans to do business with Cuban companies.

Sanguine: MEANING: Confidently optimistic and cheerful

SENTENCE: The whole family was sanguine about their chances of going on holiday.

Satiate: MEANING: Satisfy

SENTENCE: The Japanese meal did not satiate him and he ate a sandwich when he got home.

Saturate: MEANING: Soak thoroughly

SENTENCE: The rain saturated the field and caused the river to rise.

Saturnine: MEANING: Gloomy, mean, scowling

SENTENCE: Do not be misled by his saturnine appearance; he is not as gloomy as he looks.

Savour: MEANING: Appreciate fully; taste something savoury

SENTENCE: As a parent, it's important to take a step back and really savour the special moments –those children will grow up sooner than you think.

Scathing: MEANING: Very harsh or severe

SENTENCE: Joseph suffered scathing criticism from the judge at the singing competition.

Scrupulous: MEANING: Careful to do things properly or correctly

SENTENCE: She was scrupulous with repaying her friends straight away if they lent her money.

Secrete: MEANING: Conceal, hide; release

SENTENCE: HIs assets had been secreted to Swiss bank accounts

Shard: MEANING: A broken piece of a brittle artifact

SENTENCE: Shards of glass flew in all directions

Skeptic: MEANING: One who doubts others unless they have seen evidence

SENTENCE: She was sceptical about her sister's claim she had seen a ghost!

Solicitous: MEANING: Full of anxiety and concern; showing hovering attentiveness

SENTENCE: She was tiny and solicitous, a soft, sweet lady.

Soporific: MEANING: Tending to induce drowsiness or sleep

SENTENCE: The motion of the train had a somewhat soporific effect.

Spartan: MEANING: Practicing great self-denial, unsparing and uncompromising in discipline or judgement

SENTENCE: Her apartment was so spartan that she couldn't even serve us both soups; she only had one bowl and one spoon.

Spasmodically: MEANING: In spurts and fits; with spasms

SENTENCE: The newborn giraffe lies in a sodden heap, heaving spasmodically with its first gulps of air.

Specious: MEANING: Plausible but false; deceptively pleasing

SENTENCE: Misinformation, falsehoods and specious claims dominate his public pronouncements.

Sporadic: MEANING: Recurring in scattered and irregular or unpredictable instances

SENTENCE: In the last few decades, the west has been subjected to sporadic terrorist bombings.

Stigma: MEANING: A negative association

SENTENCE: These days there is far less stigma attached to being in a same sex relationship.

Stingy: MEANING: Not generous with money

SENTENCE: Many companies are too stingy to raise the salaries of their workers.

Stint: MEANING: Be very economical about spending; an unbroken period of time

SENTENCE: He doesn't stint on wining and dining – every night he spends hundreds of dollars in restaurants and bars

Stipulate: MEANING: Specify as a condition or requirement in a contract or agreement

SENTENCE: He stipulated certain conditions before their marriage

Stolid: MEANING: Showing little emotion; expressionless

SENTENCE: Her face was stolid, but inside she was thrilled.

Substantiate: MEANING: Give support to a claim

SENTENCE: More evidence of the Tooth Fairy is needed to substantiate her existence.

Superficiality: MEANING: Lack of depth of knowledge or thought or feeling; shallowness

SENTENCE: Instant digital interactions, on your phone or computer, encourage superficiality, insularity and tribalism.

Strife: MEANING: State of fighting or arguing violently

SENTENCE: Strife in the Middle East has continued for many, many years.

Supersede: MEANING: Take the place or move into the position of

SENTENCE: When his father passed away, Toby superseded him as head of the family.

Strut: MEANING: Walk with a proud swagger with a little arrogance thrown in

SENTENCE: After hitting his third six, the batsman strutted down the pitch.

Subpoena: MEANING: A writ ordering a person to attend a court

SENTENCE: The courier delivered the subpoena to her door and she had to sign for it.

Subside: MEANING: Wear off or die down; sink to a lower level; descend

SENTENCE: The world waited patiently for the danger of COVID-19 to subside.

Supposition: MEANING: An assumption or hypothesis

SENTENCE: They were working on the supposition that his death was murder.

Sycophant: MEANING: A person who tries to win favour from powerful people by flattering them

SENTENCE: The fans backstage we very sycophantic.

- T -

Tacit: MEANING: Understood, without actually being expressed; implied

SENTENCE: They were holding hands; it was tacit they were lovers.

Taciturn: MEANING: Talking little, reserved

SENTENCE: Desmond's taciturn behaviour in front of the Fulbright decision panel has made his interview awkward, hence the panel has rejected him for the scholarship.

Tangential: MEANING: Of superficial relevance, if any

SENTENCE: She made some tangential remarks on her sister's career, and then changed the subject.

Thrift: MEANING: Great care in spending money

SENTENCE: In older age, most people become thrifty and tend to save money as much as possible.

Timorous: MEANING: Timid, shy

656

SENTENCE: In big groups she was timorous, but with close friends she was very outgoing.

Tirade: MEANING: Long string of violent, emotionally charged words

SENTENCE: There are many tirades in the speeches of politicians in parliament.

Temperance: MEANING: Moderation, restraint

SENTENCE: Noted for his temperance, he seldom drinks alcohol.

Torpor: MEANING: Mental and physical inactivity

SENTENCE: After the huge meal at the fiesta, the family fell into a torpor and did not manage to dance.

Tenuous: MEANING: Very thin or slight

SENTENCE: There is a tenuous link between interest rates and investment.

Torrid: MEANING: Very hot; passionate and emotionally charged

SENTENCE: It was the most torrid romance she had ever been lucky enough to find.

Tortuous: MEANING: Full of twists and turns

SENTENCE: The route to Cairns from Brisbane in Australia is remote and tortuous.

Tractable: MEANING: Easily managed or controlled

SENTENCE: Emerging sequencing technologies can provide extra information and make the computational problem more tractable.

Transgression: MEANING: An act that goes against a law, rule, or code of conduct; an offense.

SENTENCE: I'll be keeping an eye out for further transgressions from that employee.

Trifling: MEANING: Unimportant

SENTENCE: After he interrupted the teacher with some trifling matter, the teacher resumed the class.

Truculence: MEANING: Obstreperous and defiant aggression

SENTENCE: The basketball team won through sheer truculence; there were lots of fouls in the game.

Tumultuous: MEANING: Troubled and disordered, turbulent

SENTENCE: The police presence ensured there was not a tumultuous reaction to the extension of lockdown.

- U -

Ubiquitous: MEANING: Existing everywhere at the same time

SENTENCE: Facebook, Coca-Cola and Hollywood are ubiquitous American inventions.

Umbrage: MEANING: A feeling of anger caused by being offended

SENTENCE: I took umbrage at the suggestion that I was lazy, as I work eight hours a day.

Underscore: MEANING: To emphasize, call special attention to

SENTENCE: He underscored his points in the debate.

Unseemly: MEANING: Indecent; inappropriate; unacceptable

SENTENCE: Heather's uncle made unseemly suggestions to her friend when they were alone.

- V -

Vacillation: MEANING: Moving back and forth; changing of opinion

SENTENCE: There was a fair bit of vacillation on Steven's part, he could not make up his mind.

Venerate: MEANING: Worship, adore, be in awe of

SENTENCE: You probably don't venerate your teacher or your boss, however you may act like you do!

Veracious: MEANING: Truthful; precisely accurate

SENTENCE: While we elect our leaders in the hope that everything that they say will be veracious, history has shown that such a hope is naive.

Verbose: MEANING: Using or containing too many words

SENTENCE: This article is too verbose; nobody has enough time to read the whole article, so we must edit it to make it brief and to the point.

Viable: MEANING: Able to function properly, able to grow

SENTENCE: The infant, though prematurely born, is viable and has a good chance of survival.

Vindicate: MEANING: Show to be right by providing justification or proof; clear of blame; defend

SENTENCE: The governor's policy on lockdown was vindicated by the drop in coronavirus deaths; his decision to extend it was the right one.

Viscous: MEANING: Having a thick, sticky consistency between solid and liquid; having a high viscosity.

SENTENCE: It seemed to take forever for the viscous cough medicine to pour out of the bottle.

Vituperative: MEANING: Marked by harshly abusive criticism; scathing

SENTENCE: Scots who opposed independence hurled vituperative insults at the independence party.

Vociferous: MEANING: Offensively loud; given to vehement outcry

SENTENCE: Some states in the US are contending with vociferous protests as they extend lockdown for COVID-19.

Volatile: MEANING: Liable to lead to sudden change; tending to vary often

SENTENCE: Sophie's relationship with Dave can be volatile; they fight and make up regularly.

Volubility: MEANING: The quality of being effortless in speech and writing

SENTENCE: The volubility in his expression shows his level of knowledge in the topic.

- W -

Warranted: MEANING: Justified or shown to be reasonable; provide adequate ground for

SENTENCE: The employees feel that industrial action is warranted

Wary: MEANING: Very cautious; on guard

SENTENCE: Be wary of anyone who tells you that 'anyone' can get rich with some special plan or scheme.

Welter: MEANING: Move in a turbulent fashion; a confused multitude of things; be immersed in

SENTENCE: Easter was solemnly marked amid the welter of death and suffering due to COVID-19.

Whimsical: MEANING: Determined by chance or whim; indulging in or influenced by fancy

SENTENCE: The plot and characters in *Peter Pan* are quite whimsical.

- Z -

Zeal: MEANING: Eager enthusiasm; prompt willingness; excessive fervour.

SENTENCE: Each inherited their parents' zeal for social justice.

BLANK NOTES SECTION

....

....

....

....

....

....

....

....

....

....

....

....

....

....

....

....

....

....

....

....

....

....

....

....

....

....

....

....

....

....

....

....

....

....

....

....

....

....

....

....

....

....

....

....

....

....

....

....

....

....

FREE ONLINE ENGLISH RESOURCES FOR IELTS

This is a great video activity site with clips and questions around films and TV series. It has different levels and is great for listening and speaking skills (pronunciation).

https://www.eslvideo.com/

Online Pronunciation Dictionary by Cambridge University.

https://dictionary.cambridge.org/browse/pronunciation/english/

THANK YOU

I hope you've found it useful!

As I mentioned in the foreword, a lot of hard work has gone into this project.

My whole objective with this book is to help you reach your ultimate goal of achieving an 8.5 in your IELTS test. This book is not designed to be an exhaustive list of words, but instead, a focused and easy-access guide for exam preparation. Review any sections that you feel you need to and use them as a starting point for further research and practice.

WHAT NOW?

In the next few pages, you'll find a massive bundle of free resources you can get hold of, including letter and email templates, presentation templates and grammar and vocabulary resource books! As a free member with exclusive access to my free starter library, you'll also get free reports, books and articles to help you take your English to the next level!

If you enjoyed this book, I'd be very grateful if you'd post a short review on Amazon. Your support really does make a difference and means a lot to me. I read all the reviews personally, so I can get your feedback and make this book even better in the future.

Thanks for your support.

IELTS WRITING PROFICIENCY
BAND 9 COURSE

REACH YOUR POTENTIAL IN IELTS WRITING
IMPRESS THE EXAMINER WITH YOUR

WRITING SKILLS

This is your opportunity

https://www.ieltsmasterclassonline.com
/ielts-writing-proficiency-9-course

FREE BOOK. IELTS WORKBOOK WITH 80 BASIC IELTS GRAMMAR RULES FOR 8.5

GET SMART ABOUT IELTS WRITING

Claim your FREE E-Book Worth $11.95 Below!

No Spam. Only high quality, FREE resources.

www.ieltsmasterclassonline.com

https://www.ieltsmasterclassonline.com/oto-1

Printed in Great Britain
by Amazon

22685235R00377